PENGUIN BOOKS

CABIN FEVER

Steve and Ruth Bennett have written numerous activity books, including the best-selling *365 TV-Free Activities You Can Do with Your Child* and *365 Outdoor Activities You Can Do with Your Child*. They also coauthored *Kick the TV Habit!*, which offers a complete program for altering your family's television-watching habits and contains more than a hundred TV-free activities. The Bennetts frequently share their activity ideas in national publications and on radio talk shows.

Steve is a full-time author who has written more than fifty books on parenting, environment, business management, and business computing. The former president of a technical publishing company, he holds a master's degree in regional studies from Harvard University.

Ruth is an illustrator and landscape architect who has designed public parks and playgrounds in a number of cities in the United States. She holds a master's degree in landscape architecture from the University of Virginia.

The Bennetts live with their two children, Audrey and Noah, in Cambridge, Massachusetts.

D1455297

Steve and Ruth Bennett

CABIN FEVER

202 Activities for Turning
Rainy Days, Snow Days, and Sick Days
into Great Days

PENGUIN BOOKS

PENGUIN BOOKS
Published by the Penguin Group
Penguin Books USA Inc., 375 Hudson Street,
New York, New York 10014, U.S.A.
Penguin Books Ltd, 27 Wrights Lane,
London W8 5TZ, England
Penguin Books Australia Ltd, Ringwood,
Victoria, Australia
Penguin Books Canada Ltd, 10 Alcorn Avenue,
Toronto, Ontario, Canada M4V 3B2
Penguin Books (N.Z.) Ltd, 182–190 Wairau Road,
Auckland 10, New Zealand

Penguin Books Ltd, Registered Offices:
Harmondsworth, Middlesex, England

First published in Penguin Books 1994

1   3   5   7   9   10   8   6   4   2

Illustrations by Ruth Bennett

LIBRARY OF CONGRESS CATALOGING IN PUBLICATION DATA

Bennett, Steven J., 1951–
Cabin fever: 202 activities for turning your child's rainy days,
snow days, and sick days into great days/Steve & Ruth Bennett.
p.   cm.
ISBN 0 14 02.3910 3
1. Creative activities and seat work.   2. Amusements.
I. Bennett, Ruth (Ruth Loetterle)   II. Title.
GV1203.B546   1994
790.1´922—dc20   94–18265

Printed in the United States of America
Set in Adobe ITC Garamond Light
Designed by Kate Nichols

Acknowledgments

We're grateful to many people for helping us translate this book from a cabin-fevered-inspired dream to a finished book. High on our list is our friend Stacey Miller, big kid at heart, who helped us conceptualize and develop the manuscript. Many thanks for your effort! Another playful soul, Rich Freierman, also made a great contribution to the project. Kate White, a veteran of lots of cabin-fevered days, also helped us brainstorm activity ideas. Arch Loetterle once again provided us with wonderful ideas from an era when ingenuity was the only cure for cabin fever. And special thanks go to Ben Noam for teaching us the fine points of making a comet zapper and to his mother, Maryanne Wolf, for sharing her delightfully disgusting and most secret recipe for Witches' Brew.

Our editor, Nicole Guisto, patiently awaited the manuscript and offered her usual good suggestions, while Kate Nichols and Roseanne Serra did a great job designing the book, inside and out. Caroline White helped shepherd the book through its final stages. Thanks too to Kathryn Court, publisher, for her support on the project.

We're also grateful to our agents, Lynn Chu and Glen Hartley, for their encouragement and help in making this book a reality.

Finally, we wrote this book during one of the most difficult winters of recent times, with so much snow and so many days of freezing temperatures. Our cabin-bound children, Noah and Audrey, not only patiently waited while we worked on the book but also contributed some genuine, kid-tested ideas of their own. Thanks for helping to take the edge off cabin fever in our house, Noah and Audrey. Once again, this book's a tribute to you.

Do you have any activities that you find particularly helpful in warding off or curing cabin fever? We'd love to hear them. If we use them in future editions, we'll be sure to credit your name. Send your ideas to

Steve and Ruth Bennett
P.O. Box 382903
Cambridge, MA 02238-2903

(All entries become the sole property of Steve and Ruth Bennett.)

Contents

16. Ben's Comet Zapper

17. Better Toys

18. Blindfold Games

19. Blindfold Games Revisited

20. Bocce Socks

21. Bon Voyage Party

22. Book a Vacation

23. Botanical Museum

24. Candid Camera

25. Caption (Mis) Matchup

26. Card Sharps

27. Careers

28. Celebrity Ball

29. Chain Sculpture

30. Classic Movies

31. Close-Ups

32. Clothing Store

33. Code Masters

34. Cookie Shop

35. Cooking Made Easy

36. Cordial Invitations

37. Costume Party

38. Counts in the House

39. Crazy News

40. Create a Comic

41. Desert Island Survival

42. Design a Family Brochure

43. Design a Marble Race

44. Dictionary with a Difference

45. Dramatic Readings

46. Drawing Derby

47. Drawing in Tandem

48. Dream On

49. Dual Roles

50. Durable Goods

51. Earth to Space

52. Eggtropolis

53. Embossed Art

54. Family Ad

55. Family Almanac

56. Family
Business

57. Family
Logo

58. Fantasy
Packing

59. Fashion
Show of the
Absurd

60. Find the
Pattern

61. Fine
Dining

62. Fishless
Fish Tank

63. Floor
Plan

64. Folding
Room Screen

65. For a
Better World

66. For
Reference
Only

67. Fruit
Sculpture

68. Fun in
the Sun

69. Giant
Signs

70. Gimme
Shelter

71. Godzilla
Returns
(Again)

72. Good Old
Days Book

73. Great
Gestures

74. Great
Readings

75. Greatest
Hits

76. Group Authors

77. Guess That Sound

78. Guess Where It Is

79. Guess Who

80. Hallway Pinball

81. Hat Potato

82. Hat Trimming

83. Historical Letters

84. History Buffs

85. History of Furniture

86. Holidays from the Twilight Zone

87. Home Helper

88. Home Sweet Home

89. Homemade Art-Supply Organizer

90. Homemade Piggy Banks

91. House Hunting Challenge

92. How to Walk

93. Impromptu Performances

94. In Your Child's Own Words

95. Indoor Horseshoes

96. Indoor Olympics

97. Indoor Park

98. Indoor Treasure Hunts

99. In-House Weather Reporter

100. In-Print Hunt (Older Kids)

101. In-Print Hunt (Younger Kids)

102. Instant Vacation

103. Intergalactic Gala

104. It's Great to Be . . .

105. Junior Autobiography

106. Junior Sleuth

107. Junior Soothsayer

108. Junior Technical Writer

109. Kid of All Trades

110. Kids' Guide to the Galaxy

111. Latest Fashions

112. Local Video News

113. Long Distance Pals

114. Look through Any Window

115. Made to Order

116. Magical
Moms and
Dads

117. Magical
Mystery
Machine

118. Make a
Speech

119. Make an
Ad

120. Map
Makers

121. Marble
Painting

122. Meet
Myself

123. Memory
Tester

124. Micro
Explorers

125. Mime
Switch-Off

126. Mix-and-
Match
Storybook . . .

127. Money
in the Bank

128. Mystery
Story

129.
Neighborhood
Story

130. New
Year's Eve

131. News
Radio

132. Nightlife

133. No
"Ors," "Ands,"
or "Buts"

134. Now a
Word from
Our Sponsor

135. Obstacle
Course
Bowling

136. Opinion Game

137. Organization Kids

138. Our Old House

139. Oversized Homemade Checkers

140. Paper Bag Helmets

141. Party Blower Target Shoot

142. Personal Memento Museum

143. Pet Interview

144. Pharmacy Fun

145. Phoney Phone Book

146. Picture Postcards

147. Picture This . . .

148. Ping-Pong Ball Target Bounce

149. Plot Swap

150. Poster Art

151. Presidential Pen Pal

152. Puppets in the News

153. Quick Mimes

154. Quote of the Day Holder

155. Railway Travelers

156. Rainbow Cubes

157. Reach Out and Touch Someone

158. Read the Fine Print

159. Recycled Art

160. Rosetta Stones

161. Roving Radio Reporter

162. Sales Call

163. Say It with Type

164. Scrap Stamp Painting

165. Sculpture Museum

166. Sensational Salon

167. Shoebox Topiary

168. Shooting Hoops

169. Silly Laws

170. Sing-a-Song Book

171. Smart Solutions

172. Soft Croquet

173. Sound Off in Print

174. Step Toss

175. Storybook Bingo

176.
Storybook
Treasure Hunt

177. Stuffed-
Animal Show

178.
Subminiature
Golf

179.
Superior
Supermarket

180.
Sweepstakes
Surprises

181.
Tetherball
Bowling

182. Time
Capsule

183. Toys
Galore

184.
Trailblazers

185. Tube
Heads

186. Tube
Sculpture

187. Tunnel
Vision

188. Two-Bit
Tiddlywinks

189. Two-
Dimensional
Dollhouse

190. Video
Biography

191. Wacky
Warm-Ups

192. Wall
Mural

193.
Welcoming
Committee

194. What a
Character!

195. What's
Your
Opinion?

196. White
House
Improv

197. Witches'
Brew

198. Word
Gymnasts

199. Word
Swap

200. World
Atlas

201. Your
John
Hancock

202. Zanier
Television

Introduction

Rx for Cabin Fever

The symptoms range from lethargy to bouncing off the walls. It's Cabin Fever, and it strikes every family sooner or later.

The good news is that there's a treatment, if not a cure. As the parents of two very active young children, we wrote this book to help you through those days when the snow or rain seems endless, the temperature seems permanently stuck below freezing, your child's cold or flu drags on, and your energy is on the wane. The 202 activities you'll find on the following pages will help keep your family's spirits up and your children away from the television set or video-game joystick. They've been kid- and parent-tested to ensure the most lasting relief from the "Cabin Fever Blues."

In our previous activity books, we offered projects and games designed to be done *with* your child so that you can turn whatever free time you have into quality family time. In this book, we encourage that same interaction but recognize that you can't spend every moment of a cabin-fever day entertaining or playing with your child. Many of the activities in this book require an initial setup, after which you can go about your chores and at-home work or take a little time to recharge your batteries for the next phase of the day. The activities fall into the following categories:

Arts and Crafts: Easy and fun projects that will entertain your children without requiring numerous trips to the art or hobby store; just about everything you need you'll probably find right under your nose.

Celebrations: Theme parties that you can stage to pass away the time and brighten up gray or feverish days. Good food and good company will help chase those Cabin Fever Blues away.

Create-a-Book: Activities that provide subject, text, and illustration ideas for do-it-yourself books. Provide a stack of paper and pencils, art supplies, three-ring or report binders (smaller books can be stapled together), clear adhesive covering to apply over cover art, and your child's presses are ready to roll. These activities are great opportunities for your child to use and enhance word-processing and language skills and to organize thoughts and materials into "chapters." Children who are too young to write can participate too by simply drawing the illustrations or dictating their ideas to you or an older sibling. With these activities, *everyone* can be a great author in his or her own right.

Fun and Games: A potpourri of zany ideas for using everyday objects, art supplies, or just plain talk to engage one child or a gaggle of kids with energy to spare. No, the activities in this category won't change the world but they might be just what the doctor ordered for your Cabin Fever Blues.

Great Correspondence: Activities based on writing letters to you, to other cabin-bound kids, and occasionally to a character in a book or a historical figure. Younger kids can dictate letters and decorate a cardboard mailbox; older letter writers can practice their writing and word-processing skills. And everyone can recycle the slew of envelopes included with the junk mail that you find in your box every day.

Imagine This: Fantasy, role play, and other activities that will challenge your child's creativity. Some involve high action and adventure, while others can be done during quiet play and sharing times. But all of them are a great way to beat Cabin Fever Syndrome by whisking you beyond the four walls of your house or apartment.

Indoor Sports: Action games that don't require a football stadium or a baseball diamond but are every bit as exciting as outdoor sports and a lot more appropriate for a cabin-fever day. They're designed to vent pent-up energy without jeopardizing your family's limbs or heirlooms.

Lights, Camera, Action!: Activities that use a video camera to bring out your child's creative talent. Your child can produce, direct, edit, narrate, and even star in these shows. Whether you own a camera or rent one for the day, these activities will provide terrific entertainment for everyone on the "set."

Main Street: A collection of fantasy and role-playing activities, designed to appeal to younger kids, that make it easy to "get out and about" your town. The activities range from shopping at a toy store to working as a bank teller and include all of the shops and establishments you'd expect to find on Main Street, USA.

Performances: Activities for kids and grown-ups who like to ham it up. From speeches to mimes, this category offers ideas for turning your home into the hottest theater off Broadway.

Photo Fun: Games based on finding pictures in magazines, newspaper, junk-mail pieces, catalogs, or home reference books. They cover the gamut from simple identification activities for younger children to more creative challenges for kids with reading and writing skills.

Sound Works: A collection of activities involving an inexpensive tape recorder. These activities will engage the most verbal children and challenge others to enhance their speaking skills. You're sure to capture words of wisdom that will make for price-less memories.

What You'll Need

When materials are required for an activity, you can usually find them in your kitchen, recycling bin, broom closet, or desk. Even so, you might want to start a Cabin Fever "Medicine Chest" that contains a good supply of the materials most commonly used in this book. With these raw materials on hand, you'll be able to instantly coordinate a variety of on-the-spot activities that provide immediate pleasure and entertainment and prevent cabin fever before it strikes.

To prepare for your next round of snow days, rainy days, or sick days, start collecting the following kinds of materials right away:

- Toilet paper, paper towel, and wrapping paper tubes
- Plastic containers, tubs, bottles, milk jugs, milk cartons, etc.
- Scrap aluminum foil
- Packing materials such as hard foam and peanuts (these activities are a great way to breathe new life into hard-to-recycle items)
- A supply of cardboard boxes of various sizes, some cut into sheets and some intact
- Magazines, newspapers, junk mail, catalogs, and other photo sources

In addition, when art supplies are cited as requirements in the activities, here are some of the things you'll need:

- A good stock of coloring and painting materials, including colored pencils, crayons, nontoxic markers, tempera paint, and brushes
- Nontoxic glue or double-stick tape
- Large sheets of poster board
- Drawing and construction paper
- Clear adhesive covering, such as Con-Tact brand
- Scraps of felt, yarn, ribbon, and other miscellaneous odds and ends

Finally, to do some of the indoor sports activities, you'll want to have foam balls, small rubber balls, and Ping-Pong balls on hand. A few of the activities for older kids also require marbles and balloons (see safety note below). And for activities requiring a tape recorder (those in the Sound Works category), you'll want to have some blank cassettes and earth-friendly rechargeable batteries on hand.

Safety Issues

Common sense is the key to fun and safe cabin-fever play: Just apply whatever safety rules you already have in your house for games and projects that involve cutting, gluing, and painting. Still, we want to stress that some of the activities use items and materials not appropriate for small children, such as marbles, coins, balloons, and small objects that can represent a hazard if swallowed. These activities are marked with an adult-supervision reminder. When you're playing a game or doing an activity with an older child, keep a watchful eye on toddlers who might find the materials tempting morsels.

Choosing Activities

While some activities are specifically designed for younger children (those in the Main Street category, for example) and others are geared for older kids (like those in the Lights, Camera, Action! category), most can be easily adapted to your child's age and abilities. We often explain how to modify an activity to make it easier or more difficult so that you can provide just the right level of challenge for all the participants.

Before diving into the activities, thumb through the book and scan the games and projects in various categories, noting which best match your child's interests and capabilities. Take a look at the index before you begin, too. It lists the activities by categories, as well as by useful headings such as Games and Projects Well-Suited to Bedridden Children, Quiet-Time Activities, Games and Activities for Groups of Cabin-Bound Children, and Activities for Kids Old Enough to be Home on Their Own.

And don't forget to select activities that interest you; you'll find new wrinkles on some old favorites that you probably haven't done for a while.

Curbing Competition

Finally, a note on competition for group activities. We always suggest minimizing the competitive aspect of activities, especially for younger children; they'll have plenty of time outside your home to learn how to jockey to be the "firstest" or the "bestest" or to have the "mostest." For some children, competition can add a nasty edge to otherwise enjoyable games and intensify the all-too-familiar cabin-fever "grouchies."

To downplay competition, encourage kids to try to top their own previous scores rather than yours, a sibling's, or a friend's. To this end, you might want to start a book of personal records and achievements. You might also want to redirect competitive play to cooperative effort whenever possible so that your kids direct their pent-up energy toward a shared goal rather than at each other.

Of course, some games, by definition, require a winner. But you can still stress the fact that *everyone* who plays is a winner and that the object is for everyone to have fun.

Which brings us to a final point: F-U-N *is* the only known antidote for the Cabin Fever Blues. As long as it's safe, anything goes! And go with your child's flow. Consider our activities to be springboards for creative fun and play. Encourage your child to invent his or her own rules; offer praise for devising interesting variations and for creating entirely new activities. Give yourself the freedom to be a child again too. While snow days, rainy days, and sick days can throw a monkey wrench into your plans or add a burden to an already stressful schedule, they're also an opportunity for you to stop for a moment and appreciate a tall tale about a dinosaur, role-play Winnie the Pooh, or improve your game of Bocce Socks.

Steve Bennett
Ruth Loetterle Bennett
Cambridge, Massachusetts
April 1994

CABIN FEVER

Adventure Treks

Intrepid explorers have to know how to avoid dangers like boiling-hot lava flows, alligators, snakes, crevices, and quicksand. Choose your peril; your floor is now covered with it!

Required:

Towels, sheets of paper, throw pillows, couch cushions, or old clothes

To escape the danger as well as the Cabin Fever Blues, your young adventurers need to place stepping stones across the hazards. The stepping stones can include towels, throw pillows, sheets of paper, old clothes, and sofa cushions. As the kids try to get around the house without touching the floor, they can extend their path by adding more stepping stones in strategic locations. They can also incorporate beds, chairs, and sofas as "solid ground."

Encourage your children to create an adventure story to go along with the game. Perhaps they're space explorers on a distant volcanic planet or naturalists in the alligator-infested swamps of the Everglades. Either way, they'd better try to make it safely back to their space-swamp vehicle (you might recognize it as a couch).

Whatever you do, don't fall in. . . .

Imagine This

Advertising Genius

Required:

Paper and art supplies

Why do companies spend so much money on big-ticket advertising agencies when they can turn to your child for expert advice? Show 'em your child's advertising genius with this activity.

Provide your child with markers, crayons, paints, paper, and other art supplies, then "contract" with him or her to create a name, logo, and advertisement for the following kinds of products:

- An environmentally sound automobile (the "Eco Chariot: runs on roasted peanut shells; body can be converted into compost bin, seats into lawn furniture, engine into home generator").
- A healthy, good-tasting (and environmentally correct) snack food ("Earth Bits: grown in organic soil, made from wholesome recycled tree bark; one calorie per ton, no additives, termite-free, with an edible box").
- The universal household tool, the only one you'll ever need (the "Ginzu Chore Chomper: opens cans, cores apples, polishes shoes, wakes you up, grooms pets, stirs noodles, unclogs drains; solar-powered, self-sharpening, and more!").

Imagine This

Alien Pen Pals

Your child's mission: Make friends with a creature who lives on a distant planet. Your job: Help your child set up the long-distance correspondence.

Ask your child to write (or word process) a letter to an extraterrestrial being (played by you), describing life on earth: what we look like, where we live, what we care about, what we enjoy doing, etc. Your child might also draw a picture of earthlings and record a message on cassette (so the alien can hear what we sound like), and ask questions about life on the extraterrestrial's planet. Your child can then "beam down" the letter, drawing, and tape to you and await a response.

Reply to the questions with a letter, picture, or cassette recording, and ask a few questions about life on earth that weren't answered in your child's initial correspondence. Continue the pen-pal relationship until the two of you have an in-depth understanding of your respective planets.

Perhaps you might arrange to meet for an encounter of the third kind (when we've developed our space-travel technology a bit, that is).

Required:
Writing supplies

Optional:
Tape recorder, art supplies, word processor

Great Correspondence

Almost Halloween

Required:

Cardboard, colored paper, art supplies, paper lunch bags, costume materials or ready-made costumes, treats

Your kids can't wait until Halloween to turn into pumpkins? Here's a witches' brew of fun that you can stir up anytime.

Have your child decorate the house with Halloween "props" (including cardboard pumpkins, a "witch's" broom, etc.). Then, have your child help prepare special treats for an at-home "trick-or-treat" session (perhaps you can bake cookies together). When the treats are done or cooling, have each child make a personalized "goody bag"; pass out paper lunch bags and art supplies, tape, and safety scissors for the project.

Create costumes using materials from around the house or wear ready-made costumes from former Halloweens. Then send the Halloween troop off trick-or-treating to various locations in the house such as the kitchen and living room, where you can pass out approved goodies (and set guidelines for devouring them).

Remember to keep this off-season Halloween party at home; you wouldn't want to explain to the neighbors why you're dressed up as a talking kettle and your child is garbed as a teacup!

Celebrations

Alphabet Books

If your child is a new reader (or wants to create a gift for a pre-reading sibling), an alphabet book is a perfect project and a great way to overcome Cabin Fever Syndrome.

At the top of twenty-six sheets of paper, have your child print one letter of the alphabet. Then have him or her clip interesting photos from junk mail, catalogs, or magazines, arrange them in alphabetical order, and glue them down on the appropriate sheets. Your child can take some artistic license; for example, a picture of an apple pie might be placed on the *P* page (for "pie"), the *A* (for apple pie), or the *D* (for "dessert"). In addition, your child might want to write a line or two describing the photos or even incorporate the pictures into a story.

Finally, have your child create a title page, with the name of the book and author and the date. Then "bind" the pages (using a stapler or folder) or punch holes and insert them into a notebook. Either way, give the book a place of honor in your home library.

Required:

Writing supplies, scissors, stapler, folder or hole puncher and notebook, junk mail, catalogs or magazines

Photo Fun

6 Animal Encyclopedia

Required:

Magazines, catalogs, junk mail or newspapers, art supplies, nontoxic glue or double-sided tape, binder

Here's a great way for your child to show off his or her knowledge of birds, mammals, fish, insects, and other creatures.

Have your child clip pictures of animals from magazines, junk mail, catalogs, and newspapers (or if photos are in short supply, your child can make his or her own drawings), then affix the photos to sheets of paper (one animal or group of creatures per page).

On the same or on a separate piece of paper, your child can write (or type) the important facts that he or she knows about each animal and perhaps research additional information in home library sources. He or she can also add other tidbits: personal sightings, favorite qualities, etc. An older child can describe the creature's place in the animal kingdom.

When your child finishes each report, he or she can place it in a binder, which will soon become a unique animal encyclopedia sure to rival any you'd find at the public library.

Photo Fun

Animal House

Your house is actually filled with animals. Look out, you may be sitting on one right now. . . .

With a little imagination and some paper, cardboard, and blankets, your children can turn your furniture into a wild zoo. Take your dining room table for instance, it's really an elephant. Just drape a blanket over the table and tape gray paper around each leg. Your kids can also roll up a towel and let it dangle over one end for a trunk. For finishing touches they can tape large sheets of paper to the sides to make ears.

How about a giraffe? Drape a yellow or light-colored blanket or large towel over a chair. Next, have your kids place a shoebox on top of the chair back for a head; cut a slot in the bottom of the box so it fits snugly. After they tape on some brown paper splotches, the giraffe will be complete.

Before you know it, your couch will be a whale or a dinosaur, and the footrest will be barking at you!

Required:

Construction paper, blankets or towels, cardboard box, tape, art supplies

Fun and Games

Anytime, Anyplace Airlines

Required:

Cardboard, tape or glue, yogurt-container tops, large jar tops

If the cost and inconvenience of air travel is getting you down, why not book a trip on a very private airline owned and operated by your young child?

You and your child can make a "cockpit" by affixing yogurt container tops and large jar tops to a piece of cardboard. (Or, if space and supplies are limited, your child can "fly" the plane from imaginary controls.)

Choose a destination: perhaps another state you've been to or have always wanted to visit, another country or continent.

Once you know where you're going, fasten your seat belt and take off. While "in the air," have your child tell you about the route you're taking, the landmarks you're passing, time elapsed, weather conditions, etc. And ask the person at the controls whether he or she has any ideas about the places you might see and things you might do once you land. After all, your pilot has likely flown this way many times before.

Imagine This

Arcade Target Toss

Your kids can test their athletic prowess and accuracy in this traditional arcade game, which has been domesticated for home use.

Gather up a collection of targets: Toilet paper tubes, empty milk cartons, and empty cereal boxes work great. Next, supply each player with rolled-up socks, foam balls, or Ping-Pong balls. Pick a safe spot for your arcade, such as a long hallway free of breakables. Then, using a small table or flat chair as a platform, set up the targets. Put a belt or piece of string on the floor about ten feet away to mark the throwing line. The kids should decide how many throws each player gets to knock the target down.

For variety, switch the target or the balls. Try making a pyramid of tubes and see who can knock them all down with the fewest throws.

Step up to the line! Everyone's a winner. Test your skill and maybe even win a giant stuffed animal. . . .

Required:

Rolled-up socks, foam balls or Ping-Pong balls, toilet paper tubes, empty milk cartons or empty cereal boxes

Indoor Sports

▶Adult Supervision

Required:

Wooden thread spool, matchstick, toothpick, rubber band, soap

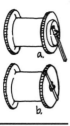

a.

b.

Fun and Games

Here's an ingenious little mobile toy that Ruth's dad enjoyed during his childhood. It's strong enough to climb up a book, but it's not motorized.

First find a wooden spool and a bar of soap. Cut off a piece of soap about the size and shape of a Lifesaver candy. Remove the flammable end of a kitchen match (your job). Place the piece of soap on one end of the spool and thread a small rubber band through the hole in the soap and spool. Insert the matchstick through one end of the rubber band to keep it from pulling through (see "a").

On the other end of the spool, cut a long recess so that when a piece of toothpick (slightly less than the diameter of the spool) is laid across the hole and is inserted through the other end of the stretched rubber band, it won't rotate (see "b"). Fine-tune your machine by experimenting with different kinds of rubber bands.

Adjust the matchstick so that part of it protrudes an inch beyond the edge of the spool. Use this end as a crank to wind the rubber band until it is taut, then place the "tractor" on the table and let it rip!

Author, Author!

Has your child read every book that his or her favorite author has written (or especially enjoyed a book by a particular writer)? Then perhaps your child would like to write the author a fan letter.

Your older child can write (or type) what he or she likes best about the author's work, feelings evoked by the book(s), lessons learned from reading the book(s), and so on. If your child has any suggestions for sequels, new endings, or characters, etc., he or she can include them as well. Your younger child might draw a picture about the book or dictate a letter to you or another "scribe."

When the letter is signed and sealed, mail it to the publisher (sometimes you'll find the address on the copyright page; otherwise, ask your librarian to see if he or she can find it for you). Publishers are usually able to forward mail to authors. Even if you don't get a response, your child will surely feel good about sharing creative thoughts and praise with someone who has been important in his or her life.

Required:

Writing supplies, envelope, postage stamp

Optional:

Computer or typewriter

Great Correspondence

12 Avant-Garde Art

Required:
Art supplies

Some of the most unusual Chinese painting came out of the Zen school, and it was often done using nontraditional techniques, like dabbing one's ponytail in pigment and then splashing it on a scroll, as moved by the "untrammeled spirit."

You might not want your kids dipping their hair in paint, but they can still have a great time creating art in an out-of-the-ordinary fashion. Break out your art supplies and see what kind of avant-garde pieces arise from your children's "untrammeled spirit" as they try the following:

- Draw or paint blindfolded
- Use the "wrong" hand to draw a picture
- Draw a picture—upside down
- Paint with a feather or piece of string
- Draw by holding the crayons or markers between palms or in the crook of the arm
- Draw together with one person blindfolded

Arts & Crafts

When the paint has dried, hang up the inspired works in the family gallery. Perhaps you're about to unveil a whole new school of art.

Balloon Decathlon

There's nothing like a lot of colorful balloons to brighten up a gray day.

Fill up a room with an assortment of balloons, then stage a balloon decathlon (remember, balloons can be a hazard for younger children). Try these "events" for starters:

▶ **Adult Supervision**

Required:
Balloons

- Keep as many balloons in the air as possible by batting or blowing at them.
- "Throw" balloons for distance.
- Have a "slow-motion" basket shooting competition (a shopping bag can be the "hoop").
- Sponsor a "javelin-throwing contest" with long balloons.
- Have the athletes lie down and try to keep the balloons in the air with their feet.
- Use a wooden spoon or paper towel tube to keep the balloons in the air.
- Have the athletes walk across the room while balancing balloons on their heads or hands.

And when the contest is over? See who can pick up and put away the most balloons in the shortest amount of time.

Indoor Sports

Beat the Clock

▶Adult Supervision

Required:

Egg timer or alarm clock, paper or plastic cups, paper plates, common household objects

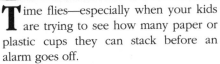

Time flies—especially when your kids are trying to see how many paper or plastic cups they can stack before an alarm goes off.

Break out your egg timer or alarm clock and try these:

- Stack-a-thon: See how many cups your kids can stack, placing a paper plate in between each, before the timer goes off. Then have everyone do the stacking with his or her eyes closed.
- Bop-a-thon: Make up a rhythm and see how many times each person can clap it off before the clock strikes zero.
- Sort-a-thon: Divvy up a collection of small items, then call out the category by which they are to be organized (e.g., square, hard, smooth).
- Sort of a Sort-a-thon: Suggest a tongue twister (like "sort of a sort-a-thon") and see how many times your kids can say it without tripping over the words within the specified time.

Finally, try slipping this one in: See if everyone can pick up the mess before the alarm goes off.

Fun and Games

Before and After

If you're of a mind to do some major housecleaning, why not capture the great results on tape?

First, enlist the help of your young videographer to "shoot" various rooms and their particular cleaning challenges. As your child takes the camera from room to room, he or she can describe how things look in their "before" state and point out what needs to be done.

Put the camera aside temporarily and have your child help you put everything in shipshape form (a great fringe benefit of this activity). Then show off your handiwork on camera: Have your child tape each room again (preferably in the same order as before) and narrate all of the improvements that have been made (pillows plumped, rugs vacuumed, closets straightened, and so on).

Whew, what a difference there is between "before" and "after." Now, how long do you think your home will stay in its new state?

Required:

Video camera, nontoxic cleaning supplies

Lights, Camera, Action!

Ben's Comet Zapper

Required:

Plastic containers, buttons, marbles or pebbles, light ball or foam football, paper or foil streamers

Even a basic target-toss game can become a high adventure if you add a bit of imagination, as our young friend Ben did for his seventh birthday.

Make targets out of clear plastic food containers, then in each one place a button, marble, pebble, or ball (this will add the sound and color). Make two side-by-side stacks of three to four targets each (these are the comets). Now you're ready to make the comet zapper by taping paper and foil streamers to a light ball such as a small foam football (it's safe for indoor use, too). When the zapper is done, have your child throw it at the comets *before* they whiz by the planet. . . .

For a more challenging game, place the targets on an overturned laundry basket with a rope attached. Slowly pull the basket across the floor while your children take their best shots.

How many throws will be necessary for your ace space explorer to blast the comets into oblivion?

Indoor Sports

Better Toys

Does your child have an idea for a great toy or an idea for improving a toy he or she currently owns? This activity will provide an opportunity to sound off.

Required:
Writing supplies, envelope, postage stamp

Suggest that your child write a letter to a toy company (look on the box or instructions for an address, then call to get the name of the appropriate person to contact at the firm). Discuss toy possibilities with your child, such as board games in which everyone wins or a badminton set that uses sponge balls so you can play it indoors.

Or perhaps a line of action superheroes who talk out their differences instead of resorting to violence.

Have your child make his or her case in a letter to the toy manufacturer and send it off. Who knows? Someday, your child's idea may hit the shelves.

Great Correspondence

Blindfold Games

▶Adult Supervision

Required:

Blindfold, socks, pots or bowls, hats, coats, gloves, coins

As kids, most of us played pin the tail on the donkey at birthday parties. But that's just one of many blindfold games that your child can do to pass the time during cabin-bound days (see next activity for more ideas).

Blindfold toss, for example, will challenge even the most athletically minded child. Place three or four pots or bowls on the floor and assign point values to each one. Blindfold your child and have him or her toss several rolled-up pairs of socks at the target containers. Then try it yourself. Perhaps the object is to get the most or least points (perhaps assign negative or "penalty" points to some containers) or to get all the socks in a bin of a certain color. It's harder than it sounds!

Once the tossing games are over, have your child keep the blindfold on, then try putting on a hat, coat, or glove (or tying his or her shoes). You try it, too.

Finally, older kids (and perhaps you) will enjoy trying to make change while wearing the blindfold. Oops, did you really mean to give away $1.50 in change for that $1.00 bill?

Fun and Games

Blindfold Games Revisited

If your child enjoyed the games in the previous activity, these are sure to be a hit.

▶Adult Supervision

Required:
Blindfold, art supplies

Put on the blindfold and break out the paper, crayons, and markers. Then let your child choose something to draw: perhaps a person, a landscape, an animal, or an object. As your child is creating the masterpiece, ask what part of the drawing he or she is working on and what colors he or she is using. You're bound to hear some amusing answers.

A variation of this activity is to call out shapes for your child to draw: For instance, draw a box inside a box inside a box or five interlocking circles. You can also call out elements of a picture: Draw a man standing on a box and holding his left arm in the air. Add a tree next to the man. Place a bird in the tree. A cloud in the sky. Who knows where the bird will wind up!

Finally, try this one on your child: Have him or her draw a clock with the hands at, say, eight o'clock. Be realistic, though; if that happens to be bedtime, your child might have difficulty drawing it even without a blindfold.

Fun and Games

Bocce Socks

Required:

Rolled-up socks, small hard rubber ball

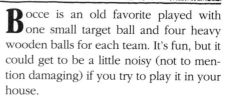

Bocce is an old favorite played with one small target ball and four heavy wooden balls for each team. It's fun, but it could get to be a little noisy (not to mention damaging) if you try to play it in your house.

For a quieter version, which can be played individually or in teams in a hallway, have your children use rolled-up socks instead of the large wooden balls; a small hard rubber ball (squash ball or racquetball) can be the target.

To begin, have one player or team roll the target to the other end of the hall. Then, starting with the other player or team, take turns tossing the socks toward the target, the object being to place the socks as close as possible to the target without touching it. Players score one point for each of their sock tosses that is closer to the target than any of the opposing team's socks (if opposing socks are touching, then there are no points). One good strategy is to use a shot to try to knock the socks of the other team away from the target.

Stay on your toes, as this game can move fast.

Indoor Sports

Required:

Paper, art supplies, snack food

What better way to escape the Cabin Fever Blues than to escape from your cabin altogether? Your kids will appreciate an exciting imaginary trip, as well as a pre-journey celebration.

Have your voyagers suggest a destination for your journey and help you plan a party using that locale as a theme. Invitations can include drawings of the spot; the date, time, and location of the party; and suggested attire.

For refreshments, your children might prepare (or pretend to concoct) such foods as you'll be eating while on vacation. For example, if you're planning a trip to the tropics, snack foods masquerading as pineapple, mango, and coconut might be the beginnings of an exciting menu.

Party-goers can also make and exchange gifts (or draw pictures of items) that might come in handy on your trip. In any case, if you're planning to travel for some time, you'll want to go all out with this celebration and make it an occasion to remember.

Celebrations

Book a Vacation

Required:

Writing and art supplies or photographs, stapler, binder or report cover

I f you'd like to make a vacation last forever, write a book about it.

Any trip that your child remembers can be turned into a story. To help your child write the narrative, ask him or her lots of questions: When did our vacation begin? Where did we go? How did we get there? What did we see? Who did we meet? and so on. You can then have your child draw pictures or use real photographs for illustrations.

Or, if your child prefers, he or she can create a book about an imaginary trip. Once your child chooses the fictional vacation spot, you can discuss the details of the place with him or her.

Either way, encourage your child to incorporate elements such as historical and current events into the story line.

Who knows, maybe the next vacation you and your child take will be at an authors' retreat.

Create-a-Book

Botautical Museum

Do you have any interesting plants or flowers at your home? Then you might just have the makings of a great botanical museum.

Have your child interview you about the care of the plants, then make placards out of thin cardboard that include the plant names, instructions for watering and feeding, unusual facts, origin, and so on. Your child can then place the identification cards in front of each plant or flower arrangement.

To expand the botanical collection, your child can draw pictures of plants, trees, shrubs, and flowers that he or she has read about or make models of them out of clay or Play-Doh. He or she should make placards for these as well.

When all the greenery is labeled, your child can announce the opening of the botanical museum and take visitors on a tour, demonstrating his or her extensive knowledge of the exhibits. Take the tour a sufficient number of times and you might learn about the secret life of plants.

Required:

House plants, thin cardboard, scissors, art supplies

Optional

Clay or Play-Doh

Imagine This

Candid Camera

Required:

Family snapshots, writing supplies

Optional:

Stick-on notes, computer or typewriter

I f you have piles of assorted snapshots taken by an ambitious family photographer, why not dust them off and put them to good use?

Have your child choose a photo (no need to remove it from an album), select a title for it, then make up a silly story to go along with it. For instance, a picture of a pet dog might be called OUR HERO, and your child might weave a tale about how the pooch rescued everyone when the dike burst and the house was swept away. Your child can write or type the story (or a prereader might dictate a story to you or an older sibling). Either way, be sure to save the narrative; years from now, it might shed some light on an obscure photo.

As a variation, you can choose a photo with one or more people (say, two children splashing in a wading pool). Then, you and your child can write "thought bubbles" on stick-on notes and affix them to the edge of the pictures. Maybe you'll find out what your children were really thinking about during that very cold swim. . . .

Photo Fun

Caption (Mis)Matchup

Sure, we may *read* the newspaper every day, but how often do we pay close attention to the pictures?

Cut out some photographs from a recent newspaper or magazine, along with the captions. Select photos from across the publication, capturing everything from the news and local sections to sports and food. Snip off and save the captions, and you're ready for some great photo fun.

Spread out the photos, then read your child the captions, pausing to see if he or she can figure out which caption goes with which picture. You'll probably learn some surprising things about the world around you!

For an interesting variation, try reading the caption and having your child draw an appropriate picture. Then pull out the actual photo so your child can compare it with his or her drawing. Which one is a better fit?

Finally, cut up and recombine both the captions and the pictures and randomly reassemble them. Read 'em and weep with laughter!

Required:

Newspapers or magazines, scissors

Optional:

Pencil and paper

Photo Fun

Card Sharps

Required:
Deck of cards

Optional:
Thin cardboard, crayons or markers

Have you ever played five-card dino-doodle? If not, don't look for the game at your local toy store; our kids made it up during a snow day. Yours can create equally exciting card games.

The easiest way to get your kids going is to hand them a standard deck of cards and have them develop some rules. Perhaps the idea is to have each person select three cards and see who can get the highest (or the lowest) total. Or, for a greater challenge, have each player select ten cards and see how long it takes one player to guess all the cards in the other's hand by drawing two cards from the deck with each turn.

For additional fun, have your children make up a set of custom cards cut from thin cardboard, using crayons or markers to make their own suits. The children can then make up their own rules or play conventional games such as Go Fish or Concentration.

Anyway, don't bet your house on that Royal Snarf; one of the other players just might have the six remaining hammerhead sharks. . . .

Fun and Games

Careers

What does your child want to be when he or she grows up? Here's how you can find out.

Required:
Writing supplies, bowl, paper bag or hat

On slips of paper, write down various job titles (use your own, your spouse's, or a friends' for inspiration). Make sure you include a variety of jobs (and feel free to include such zany positions as dinosaur trainer, bungee jumper, and haystack builder). Fold the papers in half and put them into a bowl, paper bag, or hat. Pick a job title from the hat, then act out "a day at the workplace" and see if your child can guess which job you're portraying.

Encourage your child to ask questions that will help uncover the job title: "Do you work indoors or outdoors?" "Do you work alone or with others?" "Is any special equipment required to do your job?" Then reverse roles and see if you can figure out the job title your child has chosen.

So, find any interesting possibilities for a second career?

Performances

Celebrity Ball

Required:

Paper and art supplies, snack foods, dress-up costume attire and props

Can you imagine throwing a party for your children's favorite celebrities (sports figures, dancers, musicians, inventors, historical figures, etc.)?

Your cabin-bound kids can create a guest list (by assigning each child a past or present celebrity type to role-play) and deliver homemade invitations to each other. They can then act as "costume designers" and suggest attire for each other to wear.

Have your party sponsors help you arrange the refreshments; make sure to include extravagant hors d'oeuvres (snack foods, actually) that are sure to please a high-society crowd.

Would your children like more of a challenge? Then why not have "guests" go incognito? Based on clothes, props, mannerisms, and conversation, they can take turns guessing the name of each celeb.

Be sure to listen to the party conversation when your famous guests start mixing with one another. What do you suppose the First Lady will say to the opera singer?

Celebrations

Would you like to get your kids to team up on a creative project? How about a group effort at a sculpture?

Give your children clay or Play-Doh to work with, and have them collaborate on a single sculpture. You can give each of them different colors or simply keep the supply of raw materials handy for all of them to use. Each child takes turns adding pieces so that the sculpture gradually takes form.

Required:

Clay or Play-Doh

Your kids can pick a subject for the sculpture before they start, then work together to complete it, or each child in turn can decide what the sculpture should look like at the moment and add whatever piece he or she feels is appropriate. You can also have them guess the idea behind each other's additions to the sculpture as they proceed.

Yet another alternative is to have each child start a separate sculpture without announcing what it is, then switch after a few minutes to add to or complete the work of other "artists." No doubt these creations will take on a whole new meaning in someone else's hands!

Arts & Crafts

Classic Movies

Required:
Video camera

Some say the best movies were those made before the advent of sound and color (in the theater, that is). Why not have your child produce his or her own silent, black-and-white "film" (videotape, actually)?

First decide on a genre (a western, comedy, drama, etc.). Then cast the roles (you and your child might each play more than one part, or you can enlist the help of other family members). The "actors" should dress in black, white, and gray garments (if you can find old hats, boots, and jackets to fill out the wardrobe, even better).

Have your child invent a simple plot: Perhaps the villain has tied an innocent victim to the railroad tracks (a runner in your hallway). Your child (or whoever is directing the piece) can then tell the actors to take their places and call "Action!"

Lights, Camera, Action!

From then on, the actors mime all the actions until the director says "Cut!" The director can then set up a new scene and begin again. When the "shoot" is finished, play back the movie and let everyone watch the plot unfold. Quiet on the set!

Close-Ups

Kids are often amazed when they first use a magnifying glass on familiar objects: "My hand looks like that?" is a typical comment. You can easily harness that excitement for a bit of cabin-fever-busting fun by having your child try the following kinds of observations.

Required:

Magnifying glass (preferably with plastic lens)

Optional:

Paper and pencil, art supplies

- Magnify some interesting objects (an orange, leaf, toys, etc.) and have your child draw pictures of the enlarged items.
- Have your child report on the fine print on currency, coins, and advertisements.
- Write your child a message in tiny letters and have him or her "decode" it with the magnifying glass.
- Have your child examine textures in the walls, floors, drapes, etc., then comment on what can't be seen with the naked eye.

As your child will tell you, there's so much just waiting to be discovered right under your nose if you know how to look.

Fun and Games

Clothing Store

Required:

Clothes and accessories, large sheet of cardboard, egg carton or shoebox, play currency, sheet, writing supplies

How would you like to visit a fashion boutique that features all the latest styles?

Help the "buyer" (your child) gather an assortment of clothes from your collection. Be sure to include a variety: casual and formal wear, fashions for different seasons, accessories, etc. Your child can then arrange the "merchandise," along with a mirror (made of cardboard), a dressing room (drape a sheet over a closet door), price tags, and "for sale" signs.

Then have your child "sell" you some items (of course, you can try them on and get the "salesperson's" opinion). When you've made your choices, have your child ring up the purchases on his or her cash register (an egg carton or shoebox filled with play currency). Now switch places with your child: See whether you can persuade your child to buy some "new" clothes for him- or herself.

You just can't beat the convenience of at-home shopping!

Main Street

Code Masters

If your older child enjoys cracking codes and solving riddles, he or she will definitely find this activity appealing.

Required:
Writing supplies

The idea is to write phrases or sentences using a combination of words and pictures but leaving out a key word for your child to solve. For instance, the maxim "Waste not Want not" might be written as follows:

Here's another adage (A penny saved is a penny earned):

To get into the spirit of things, try this one (A stitch in time saves nine):

Fun and Games

Cookie Shop

Required:

Baking ingredients and equipment, writing supplies, chalkboard or cardboard

Optional:

Art supplies, beverages

Main Street

Do you and your child have a sweet tooth and some baking skills? Then you'd probably enjoy operating an at-home cookie shop.

Before you can open the business, you'll need to create some "inventory." Help your child bake some family favorites (this is also a great opportunity to try some new recipes). You might also choose to "stock" other snacks (brownies, granola bars, muffins, etc.) and drinks (hot chocolate, juice, milk, and so on).

Your child can create a menu (using a chalkboard, cardboard, or other suitable materials) with the names and prices of the offerings. Of course, he or she can include a brief description of each (for example, "mouth-watering oatmeal bars made with natural fruit").

Finally, have your child arrange the wares in the "showcase" (the kitchen or dining room table), then hang up a store sign to announce the shop is open for business. That and the smell of fresh-baked goods ought to entice droves of "customers" to sample your wares.

Cooking Made Easy

This recipe for fun calls for one video camera, a pinch of imagination, and plenty of kids' favorite foods.

Have your children create a cooking show based on the preparation of their favorite meals. Topics include assembling the perfect taco, mastering the triple-decker peanut butter and jelly sandwich, proper placement of chips on the sandwich plate, and how to peel a hard-boiled egg.

Once your children have decided on a topic and planned their show, help them set up at a counter or table that's at a good height for them to work.

Encourage your children to give as detailed an explanation as possible in the presentation; they can pretend they're explaining the recipes to someone from another country or even another planet. Alternatively, your children can concoct ridiculous recipes out of real or imagined ingredients.

Step aside, Galloping Gourmet, here come the Catering Kids.

Required:
Video camera, cooking ingredients for favorite recipes

Lights, Camera, Action!

Cordial Invitations

Required:

Art supplies

Optional:

Cardboard box, envelopes

When was the last time you got an important invitation? Well, your child is about to change all that.

Provide your child with a variety of arts and crafts supplies: drawing paper, markers, paints, crayons, glue, construction paper, yarn, buttons, felt, etc. Then, put him or her to work creating special invitations.

Your child can make "invites" to an actual upcoming event: a tetherball bowling tournament (see activity 181), a comet-blasting session (16), a fun-in-the-sun celebration (68), or the opening of a new toy store (183). Your child can also create invitations for spectacular happenings that he or she invents, such as the groundbreaking for a new skyscraper in your backyard or the official commemoration of Groundhog Day.

Have your child "send" out the invitations (perhaps place them in a cardboard family mailbox), including RSVP cards if desired; after all, you and your guests will surely want to firm up your plans.

Fun and Games

Costume Party

Take old clothes, paper bags, pillow-cases, and fabric markers. Glue on sparkles for accent or decorate with a pinch of feathers. Throw in a generous dollop of imagination and your children have the makings for a hilarious costume party! Try these costume ideas as starters:

Required:

Old clothes, pillowcases, play hats and belts, fabric markers, scissors

Optional:

Trimmings, nontoxic glue, masks or disguise props

Whole body costumes. Have your kids decorate old pillowcases and add belts, bells, and trim for a final touch. Cut holes for your kids to see.

Goofy hats. Long-sleeve toddler shirts make fun hats for older kids. Stuff them with tissue or newspaper to make the arms stand up.

Headless wonders. A large shirt buttoned over a child's head can provide the basics for a headless monster.

Coming and going. By putting clothes and hats on backward and adding play eye-glasses or a mask to the backs of their heads, your children will be coming and going at the same time.

Now, aren't your kids the best dressed in town?

Arts & Crafts

Counts in the House

Required:

Writing supplies, binder or notebook

Here's an activity idea that you can always count on to challenge your child. It involves having him or her tell you how many items there are in your home or room that fall into various categories (things to sit on, things that move, green things, square things, and so on).

A younger child can walk around your house or apartment and actually count the items. An older child can try to recall how many objects there are in a category from memory (an activity that can be a challenge for a grown-up as well).

As a variation, pose a "house-counts challenge": you and your child (and any other players) each take a guess at how many flowers there are on the kitchen wallpaper, how many pink tiles there are on the bathroom floor, etc. When all guesses are in, have your child take an official count and see whose answer was closest.

Fun and Games

Your child can keep a Master Record notebook that lists all of the house counts. Each entry should include a date and the counter's name. No doubt this will be a great family archive in the years to come.

Crazy News

If you're tired of reading the same kind of newspaper and magazine stories every day, here's an opportunity to liven things up by having your kids "write" (cut and paste) their own articles.

First, have your child clip several stories and headlines from periodicals (you might want to edit them first for content), then he or she can cut the articles into paragraphs. The next step is to reassemble the paragraphs, adding connecting sentences to link the ideas. Finally, apply headlines. Take turns reading the new "articles" aloud, trying to do so without cracking a smile.

Be sure to combine parts of articles from different sections (say, the cover-story headline, a prediction from the horoscope page, and an article from the food section). You can affix pictures as well, mixing and matching captions to add to the zaniness.

Isn't it amazing that yesterday's baseball game was rained out because a visiting head of state took a detour into a bowl of homemade clam chowder? There's a picture of him on his way home in the space shuttle. . . .

Required:

Magazines and newspapers, scissors, double-stick tape or nontoxic glue

Photo Fun

Create a Comic

Required:

Magazines, junk mail or catalogs, card stock or poster board, double-stick tape or nontoxic glue, scissors

Optional:

Marker, straightedge

Photo Fun

Does your child enjoy following the "funnies" in your local newspaper? Then he or she would probably enjoy making an original comic strip.

Have your child clip pictures from magazines, catalogs, and/or junk mail (people, pets, food, electronic gadgets, etc.), then arrange the photographs while deciding on captions or thought/speech "bubbles." The captions can be simple text (for instance, a smiling child might bear the caption MAKE A FRIEND), while the thought bubbles might be humorous musings (a cat, for instance, might be thinking, "Gee, maybe the doorbell will ring as soon as they open that can of tuna fish").

When your child has finished arranging the pictures, provide glue or double-stick tape so he or she can affix them in their proper places on a piece of card stock or poster board. Older children might want to box the "frames" with a straightedge and marker and write a title for the whole strip.

Offer lots of praise and encouragement; your child just might have a brilliant career as a comic-strip artist.

Desert Island Survival

Imagine this: You and your child are marooned on a desert island. All you have are the clothes on your back, whatever materials you can find, and your wits. How will you survive?

Required:

Sofa cushions and towels, string, yardstick, rubber bands, blocks

First, you'll need a place to spend the night. Have your child help you build a shelter out of rocks and leaves (sofa cushions, towels, etc.; see activity 70 for suggestions). When you get hungry, the two of you can search for fruit trees, roots, and berries (perhaps provide some actual food for the activity; all this play can build up quite an appetite). Or you can make fishing poles out of tree limbs and vines (string and a yardstick), bait the hooks with fruit or insects (rubber bands), and see what you can catch.

If you get cold, you can build a fire after you and your child collect a pile of wood (blocks). And, once the blaze is roaring, the two of you can plan enough exploration and imagination activities to keep you busy until help arrives.

Relax, civilization is just a search party away.

Imagine This

Design a Family Brochure

Required:

Pencil and paper

Optional:

Family snapshots, small cardboard box

Arts & Crafts

Who says that only businesses can have fancy brochures touting their virtues? Why not have your child create one for the family?

The "brochure" (a piece of paper folded in halves or thirds) could start off with a general blurb about the family: "We're the Smiths and we live at 22 Main Street. We like to go for hikes and cook out in the backyard." Your child might want to include a family logo and tag line (see activity 57) to spice up the brochure.

After the opener, your child can write (or dictate to you or an older sibling) descriptions of family members: their likes and dislikes, greatest achievements, funniest moments, favorite possession, dreams and aspirations, and so on. He or she might want to interview siblings or you to get some first-hand quotes. If possible, provide photographs that your child can tape to the brochure.

When completed, the brochure can go into a display unit (a small cardboard box) that you keep by the door; future guests can pick it up on the way in to get a better idea of what's in store for them during a visit to your home.

Design a Marble Race

All your kids need for a day at the races are some marbles and cardboard tubes.

Use a hallway or room with a wooden or linoleum floor for the racetrack. Have your children hold one end of the cardboard tube in the air while keeping the other end on the floor to form a marble launching "jetway." Each player simply releases the marble at the top of the tube to send it on its way. (Supervise closely if young siblings are watching the play. Also, if young children are playing the game, try using tubes that are large enough to accommodate Ping-Pong balls.)

The simplest race is to see who can get a marble across a finish line first. Your children can make the race more challenging by including a simple target at the finish line (say, a small piece of folded paper standing on edge). Or, they can try to have their marble stop as close as possible to the finish line by raising or lowering the ends of their tubes to control the speed.

Players ready? Marbles ready? They're off!

▶**Adult Supervision**

Required:

Marbles (or Ping-Pong balls), cardboard tubes

Optional:

Paper or other targets

Fun and Games

Dictionary with a Difference

What's in a word? Find out with this activity.

Help your child make a dictionary that contains his or her own vision of what words mean. First, divide a sheet of paper into two columns. On the left side, list common words (such as *cup, baseball, envelope,* and *notebook*). Then, on the right side, have your child write definitions that describe the objects (for example, "something to drink out of, like a glass, but it has a handle").

For older children, you can cull longer words (especially technical or scientific terms) from a dictionary (such as *forestation, recombinant, trinitrotoluene, constrained, tachistoscope,* etc.). Your child can then write the actual definitions if he or she knows them or invent meanings. For a more complete dictionary, he or she can draw illustrations that accompany the definitions and use each word in a sentence: "The dinosaur's shoes *constrained* her dancing."

So, how long do the passengers wait at *forestation* before the bus leaves for the city?

Create-a-Book

Dramatic Readings

Do your children enjoy performing more than they do rehearsing? Then challenge them to a "cold" dramatic reading of just about anything.

Required:

Books, newspapers, and other reading matter

First, designate a speaker. Then, have him or her stand at the "podium" (the back of a chair). Hand the speaker a pre-selected passage from a book, magazine, or newspaper and listen to an impromptu dramatic reading.

For more fun, you can choose reading material that's difficult to dramatize: an entry or two from a dictionary or encyclopedia, a page from a math textbook, the stock columns of a newspaper, a passage from an instruction manual, the label on a can or box of food, entries from a junk-mail catalog, or listings from the residential or business telephone directories.

Could *you* render a weather forecast in the newspaper as though it were written by one of the great poets of all time?

Performances

Drawing Derby

Required:
Art supplies

Here's how you can turn simple draw-ing into a fun group activity and a good Rx for the Cabin Fever Blues.

Set up a table with a sheet of paper and a chair for each child and have plenty of markers or crayons on hand. Next, have your kids suggest enough drawing topics so that there's one for everybody. Label each sheet of drawing paper with a sepa-rate topic. (As an alternative to separate sheets, you can cover the entire table with one large sheet of paper.)

Once all the kids are ready with a blank sheet and a drawing topic, have them start drawing. After a short time (about one minute) have everyone stop drawing, move one seat to the right, and continue with the picture at that seat. Keep going until all the kids have con-tributed something to each drawing.

For a variation, you can give each child one or two markers so that they all have different colors, and have them keep their markers with them as they move. That way, they can look back at all the pictures and identify which part they added.

On your mark, get set, draw!

Arts & Crafts

Drawing in Tandem

Are you on the same artistic wavelength as your child? Find out with this activity.

Required:
Art supplies

Supply yourself and your child with pieces of paper, as well as crayons, markers, or colored pencils. Find a place where the two of you can draw without seeing each other's paper, then take turns calling out shapes to be drawn. When you're finished, compare pictures, and see how alike or dissimilar they may be.

A variation on the activity entails combining shapes, objects, and colors. For instance, the following sequence of drawing tasks—"square," "green," "tree," "car," "circle," and "yellow"—might lead one person to draw a picture of a house with a green front lawn, a tree in front, a car parked in front of the house, and a yellow sun in the sky. The other person might have drawn a statue of a car on a pedestal next to a large green tree with a round brass plaque on the base.

Want to get real tricky? Toss in some abstract things to illustrate, such as "love," "happiness," and "fear." You might be surprised at the window this opens into your child's mind (and your own).

Arts & Crafts

Dream On

What do cats, dogs, bunnies, frogs, and other critters dream about? Science may never tell, but your kids will enjoy whiling away the time with their speculations.

Suggest an animal—say, a lion—and ask your child to put him- or herself in the animal's paws, demonstrating a knowledge of a lion's secret wishes: "I dreamt that all the humans went food shopping and bought lots of meat. They got home and unpacked the food, but before they could put it away, they froze in place long enough for me to make a meal out of it." For a group of cabin-bound kids, one person suggests an animal, then each one suggests a dream or builds on a dream that's already been started.

Try spinning a dream for an actual animal, like your own household pets, your friends' or neighbors' pets, or the dog you meet on the way to work or school every day, taking into account their unique personalities. Then, with those same characters in mind, come up with a silly nightmare for them as well: "I was the only cat at a German shepherd party. . . ."

Imagine This

Dual Roles

How would your child like to fulfill an actor's dream: to play Romeo and Juliet at the same time?

Have your child find a two-person scene from a play (or you and your child can write a page or two of original dialogue). Now you're ready to record. Have your child read the first character's opening lines, pausing afterward to allow enough time for the second character's response; if there are any actions that go along with the lines, such as entering a room, be sure that your child allows enough time for them as well. Your child can continue recording the first character's lines (and pausing at the right times) until the scene is concluded.

Now rewind and play the tape, with your child offering a "live" rendition of the second character's lines. If your child timed his or her first reading correctly, then he or she should have just enough time to respond to the appropriate cues.

It might take a bit of practice to get it just right, but actors are used to rehearsing a scene extensively before it's ready for Broadway.

Required:

Tape recorder, script for play

Sound Works

50 Durable Goods

Required:

Clear adhesive covering, art supplies

Arts & Crafts

C lear adhesive covering is one of the greatest inventions of all time. Here are some ideas for its use that will allow you and your child to create useful items that will last for years.

Placemats. Give your child some drawing paper and have him or her decorate each sheet (both sides) with food, flowers, or abstract designs. Label each placemat with a family member's name and cover the back and front with clear adhesive, ensuring that each has a complete seal.

Bookmark. Cut drawing paper to size (say, eight inches by two inches). Then have your child decorate it with original art. Cover it with clear adhesive and punch a hole through the top. Thread a length of ribbon through the hole and hit the books!

Ornaments. Cut circles, stars, and other shapes out of drawing paper or cardboard and decorate both sides. Apply clear adhesive covering, and tie a piece of string through a hole in the top. *Voilà!* A hanging masterpiece.

This doesn't even begin to cover the possibilities. . . .

Earth to Space

If your child is planning to blast off into space in the near future, why not capture your two-way radio transmissions on tape?

Required:

Tape recorder

While your child is traveling, turn on the tape recorder and document all of your conversations with the junior astronaut. Find out whether the takeoff went smoothly, what your child sees out the windows, what he or she is wearing, and so on. Also, have your child tell you the spacecraft's destination and what he or she expects to find there.

When your child arrives, have him or her tell you all about the landing site: what the weather is like, whether there are any living creatures (perhaps your child can interview one), what kind of food there is to eat, etc. Then contact your child again on his or her trip home; if possible, stay in touch until he or she lands safely.

These taped conversations are the earthlings' only way of hearing about this space trip, so be sure the astronaut clearly transmits all the important news!

Sound Works

Eggtropolis

Required:

Egg cartons, small cartons, food boxes, scissors, art supplies, poster board, magazines and other photo sources

Here's how your children can make a cityscape out of milk cartons, shoeboxes, and egg cartons (with holes in the top).

First, cut a sheet of poster board in half lengthwise and tape the ends together to create a backdrop for the city. Next, have your children create buildings out of the egg-carton tops (the holes are the windows) and various-sized boxes. Each one will be glued to the backdrop so only the front and sides show, and your children can use the cartons in different ways to create a variety of buildings.

Have your children draw or cut out pictures of people to place in windows in the buildings before they are glued down and use paint, colored paper, and other materials to decorate the surrounding structures.

As each building is completed, have your children affix it on the background. They can then add pictures from magazines and junk mailings to complete the scene, such as birds or airplanes above the buildings and people walking in front.

Arts & Crafts

Sounds like a city planner's dream to us.

Embossed Art

Embossed pictures are an art form in themselves. With this activity, your child can emboss right in your kitchen without expensive printing gear.

Have your child draw or trace the outline of an animal, a car, a leaf, or a geometrical form on a piece of thick corrugated cardboard. The cardboard should be at least the same dimensions as the paper you'll be using, preferably an inch larger on each edge. Cut out the shape with a sharp knife (your job).

Now take a piece of white paper and mist it with a plant sprayer. Apply just enough water so that the paper is malleable (if it's too wet, it will fall apart).

Lay the paper over the cutout and *gently* push it into the recess, following the cutout edge with your finger. Next, place several thicknesses of a cloth towel over the paper to absorb water. Place a heavy object on top so that the paper remains in the cutout as the water evaporates.

When the paper is dry, remove it from the cardboard and *presto!* an embossed piece of artwork that your child can turn into a greeting card or a piece of art suitable for framing.

Required:

Corrugated cardboard, white paper, towel, plant sprayer

Arts & Crafts

Family Ad

Required:

Art supplies, glue

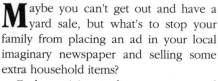

Maybe you can't get out and have a yard sale, but what's to stop your family from placing an ad in your local imaginary newspaper and selling some extra household items?

Each participant chooses a personal or family possession and writes, types, or word-processes an advertisement. Begin each ad with an attention-getting headline, and follow up with copy that touts the virtues of the object.

You'll also want to include the price, a description, and other details. An older child can later take the ads and turn them into a "classifieds" page by taping or gluing them onto a sheet of drawing paper (check your local newspaper for some style ideas). Items you and your fellow ad-writers might sell include toys and books, furniture, household appliances, clothes, or sports equipment.

Fun and Games

You might also want to include some "unsellable" items that are "kicking around the house," such as the Brooklyn Bridge, dinosaurs, the moon, a mountain, the sky, or Niagara Falls. How much do you think you can get for the goose that lays the golden eggs?

Family Almanac

If your home library doesn't yet include a book about your family, then why not have your child make one or more?

Your child can write a fictional story that includes all family members in the plot. Other characters, real or imaginary (such as friends, neighbors, pets, etc.), can also be woven into the narrative. Or your child can chronicle a family event that really happened (the birth of a younger sibling, moving to a new home, visiting out-of-state relatives, and so on).

In addition to (or instead of) writing a storybook, your child can create a reference book about your family. He or she might include information about each family member such as likes and dislikes, accomplishments, academic record, best personality traits, and plans for the future.

Once your child's literary work is finished, arrange to have the whole family read it together. This is one book that will speak volumes.

Required:
Writing supplies, stapler, binder or report cover

Create-a-Book

Family Business

Required:

Art supplies, boxes, small household items

How would you and your children like to do something productive with your free time? Starting a small family business is sure to generate some fun, if not hard cash (or fodder for your resumé).

First, decide what type of company to open (if your children are stumped, you might suggest the business in which a favorite relative or family friend works).

Next, make some props: a cardboard-box computer or cash register, boxes for "inventory," items from around the house as demos, and so on. Have your kids "mint" some money from colored paper and crayons or markers; perhaps they can create some sales slips or receipts as well. Then suggest roles that everyone can play; some kids can be employees of the firm while others can be customers.

However you play, this is an opportunity to show the world what real customer satisfaction is all about.

SPECIAL TODAY
NAILS 5¢
SCREWS 2
WOOD 10¢

Imagine This

Family Logo

If your child is a budding graphic artist, offer him or her the ultimate challenge: Create a logo that captures the essence of your family.

Required:
Art supplies

Give your child some art supplies (drawing paper, crayons, paint, pencils, and so on) and an assignment to come up with a design that "says it all" about your family. Perhaps your child can draw a picture that communicates a mood (happiness, togetherness, playfulness) or an event (holidays, apple-picking, dancing, etc.).

When your child has created the perfect visual image, have him or her write a tag line, a sentence, or phrase that describes or adds more information to the picture. For instance, your tag line might be "A Family That's for the Birds" or "We're Green Thumbs Up."

Your child can use the logo and tag line to create family stationery, envelopes, greeting cards, postcards, newsletters, and all manner of printed materials; simply take his or her camera-ready original to a local copy shop. The possibilities are limitless.

Arts & Crafts

Fantasy Packing

Required:

Shopping bag or play suitcase, recycled materials, writing supplies, art supplies, everyday items and clothing

H alf the fun of taking a trip is often in the planning, especially about what to take along. And there's *never* enough room for everything your children want to bring. Can you imagine how tricky it would be to have them pack for a trip to a faraway place, even another planet?

To play this game, give each of your children a shopping bag or play suitcase and tell them to get ready for a trip. Limit the number of items they can bring to ten or so and tell them that they won't be able to buy any other supplies while they are on their journey. Have them pick a fantasy destination, then tell them to get packing!

Your children can pick everyday items they think they might need, or they can invent the perfect tools and magical machines to bring along by piecing together recyclables or by drawing them. After all participants have packed their bags, take turns explaining what the different items are and why they were selected.

Remember, don't leave home without it, whatever *it* is.

Imagine This

Fashion Show of the Absurd

Who says you need a certain look to be a fashion model? With this activity, even the family pet can get in on the act.

Required:
Clothes and accessories

Your child or a group of cabin-bound kids can put together unusual ensembles and strut down the "runway" (a hallway). You can play the master of ceremonies, providing general commentary on the show and describing various outfits, such as:

The Turn-It-Around Look—a backwards T-shirt fashion show

Double Splendor—a mismatched-socks fashion show

Fits Like a Glove—socks on hands, gloves on feet

The Clash Bash—out-of-sync patterns

Rainbow Riot—something in every color

The Crazy Cuff Look—rolled-up sleeves, pant legs, socks, etc.

Yes, folks, these models are *simply lovely, just lovely!* And they're coming to a living room in your town soon.

Fun and Games

Find the Pattern

Required:

Magazines, junk mail, catalogs or newspapers

How many patterns can you and your child find in, or make from, pictures?

Have your child sort photos from magazines, newspapers, junk mail, and catalogs into various categories. Younger children might stick to general groups such as people, green objects, or squares. Older kids can get a bit more sophisticated (say, arranging people by profession, objects by where or how you use them, etc.). Your child can then challenge you to name the theme of each group or ask you to add an appropriate photo.

As a variation, you can use photos to create a pattern with one object missing and see if your child can figure out what kind of picture should fill in the blank. For example, you might line up the photos alphabetically by the main subject, then remove one, and see if your child can find a photo that would fit the bill. Switch roles and see if your child can create a pattern that will stump you.

So, do you see a pattern yet to all this fun? Simple, it's creativity.

Photo Fun

Fine Dining

Which is the nicest restaurant in the world? The one at your house, of course.

Have your child transform your house into a fine dining establishment complete with tablecloths, special place settings, flower arrangements, menus, and so on. Provide paper and art supplies to create the menu; a younger child can dictate menu choices while an older one can write up his or her own.

Your child can play a variety of roles, from maître d' and waiter to chef and wandering musician. Suggest that he or she serve up the courses (imaginary or snack foods) in the most appetizing and artful way possible. Be sure to set up a "kitchen" near the dining table with pots and pans so you can take in the great aromas as the chef whips up exotic concoctions.

Finally, a group of children can alternate roles so that each gets to be the waiter; after all, it's only fair that they share in the big tips.

Required:

Paper, art supplies, dinnerware and pots and pans

Optional:

Play dishes or paper plates, snack foods

Imagine This

62 — Fishless Fish Tank

▶Adult Supervision

Required:

Clear plastic bowl or container, art supplies, marbles, pebbles and/or seashells, sponge, green trash bags, foam peanuts or soap, toy boats, etc.

If your child has always wanted to have an aquarium at home, here's how you can make a low-maintenance version.

Start with a large, clear plastic bowl or container. Then have your child draw an aquatic background (with plants, rocks, coral, fish, etc.) on a sheet of paper and tape it to the back of the bowl (or around part of the back for a round bowl). Decorate the bottom of your fish tank with marbles or pebbles (watch young children), seashells from last summer's vacation, and strips of green trash bags and sponges for underwater plants. Then add water (three-quarters of a "tank").

Now have your child add the "fish" (hard foam peanuts and slivers of soap). You can also add toy boats, scuba divers, and so on. To watch the fish and other items "swim," simply stir the water around with your finger or a spoon.

Have your child name the fish and establish a feeding schedule; perhaps the fish require a pinch of food (salt) twice a day. Feeding time is also great for engaging in that other terrific cabin-fever buster:

Fun and Games

telling fish stories.

Floor Plan

Here's a simple drawing project that will get kids to take a closer look at familiar surroundings: their dwelling.

Required:
Writing supplies, ruler

All you need for this activity is a pencil, a ruler, and some paper (graph paper works best) on which your child can draw a map of the inside of the house or apartment.

First, have your child measure the length and width of each room by "kid steps," counting each complete pace (that is, left foot, right foot) as one step. Help pick a scale that allows for an entire floor of the house to be drawn on one sheet of paper (say, two squares on the graph paper are equal to one kid step). It's also helpful if your child draws each room as he or she measures it, rather than trying to do it from memory.

When the floor plan is done, your child can draw in furniture and color each room to match the real thing. Don't forget to suggest adding the most important part of the house: the people who live there.

Arts & Crafts

Folding Room Screen

Required:

Cardboard, duct tape (if cardboard is separate sheets), art supplies, magazines and other picture sources, sheets of paper

This folding screen is something your kids will have fun making and using for a long time.

To make the basic screen, use three or four large pieces of heavy cardboard; the sides from an appliance box work very well. If the box is intact, cut open one corner so that the sides are still connected and fold it accordion-style so that it stands up. If your children are starting with separate pieces of cardboard, make connecting hinges with strips of duct tape.

Now you can have your children decorate their folding screen using paints, markers, and pictures clipped from magazines (depending on the type of decorations they chose to apply, your children may want first to cover the cardboard with sheets of paper more suitable for coloring).

When the screen is done, your children can use it to enclose a reading nook or perhaps to designate where the playroom ends and the shores of a getaway tropical island begin.

Arts & Crafts

For a Better World

Here's a way to pass the time and get your child thinking about some important issues of the day.

Hand your child an object and ask how we might use it to help the immediate and larger community. (Older kids may want to write up their answers; you can also tape them on a cassette recorder for posterity). For instance, a pair of barbecue tongs could pick up litter in the park. Eggbeaters might be used to make meals for everyone in the world. A bucket would catch rainwater for use in the garden. A crayon might make an important poster. Shoes would allow the wearer to walk somewhere instead of driving.

You can enhance the game by passing the object back and forth and building on your child's vision. The tongs used to clean up the park could multiply along the block so that neighbors could take turns keeping their street clean.

No, we can't save the world with tongs or eggbeaters, but this activity will inspire your child to think about the creative possibilities for a better future.

Required:

Common household items

Optional:

Tape recorder, writing supplies

Imagine This

Required:

Reference books, pencil and paper, stapler, binder or report cover

If your child enjoys exploring the information in encyclopedias, perhaps he or she is ready to write and illustrate an original volume.

Have your child develop a list of categories such as people (inventors, scientists, presidents, etc.), science and nature (eclipses, tides, tornadoes, and the like), arts and literature (theater forms, musical instruments, and so on). Then, within each category, have your child decide which individual subjects to include.

If you have encyclopedias, dictionaries, and other reference materials available, your child can research information and study illustrations as inspiration for those he or she will create for an original volume. Contribute what you know about the subject as well.

For a variation, your child can create whimsical entries using his or her imagination; perhaps the book is *Michael's Awesome Un-Encyclopedia.* You might be surprised to learn that Carry Nation was actually the person who invented baseball, according to your resident expert. . . .

Create-a-Book

Fruit Sculpture

Here's an activity that allows your child to create a face with history written all over it.

First peel and core an apple, removing any bruises. Then have your child use a butter knife to create facial features (supervise closely). You might want to give your child a head start by defining a rough outline first.

When your child has finished carving the apple, place it in a bowl of salty water for an hour, then remove and blot it with a paper towel.

Insert a chopstick or Popsicle stick into the bottom of the carved apple and rest it in a tall plastic soda bottle weighted down with coins or marbles (watch young children). As the apple dries, it will shrivel, and the face will constantly change over the course of several days or more. Encourage your child to make paper or felt clothes that can be taped to the bottle or cup, then make up a story about the apple person.

Just contemplate the possible story lines; they're all fruit for thought.

▶Adult Supervision

Required:
Apple(s), peeler, butter knife, salt, plastic bottle, coins or marbles

Optional:
Paper or felt, tape

Arts & Crafts

Fun in the Sun

Required:

Summer garb, blankets

Optional:

Cardboard boxes, refreshments, balloons, cooler and beach gear, dishpan, rice or small noodles, toy boats, etc., pictures of the beach and ocean

Celebrations

How would you like to enjoy an indoor beach party in the winter or any time of the year?

Of course, you'll want to dress appropriately, so have family members dig out and change into their bathing suits, hats, sunglasses, sandals, etc. Your child can help you gather supplies you'll need (blankets, a cooler, beach chairs, and so on) and spread them on the "shore."

Next, turn your playroom (or other room) into your own private "beach." You might display toy boats, hang up pictures of the ocean, or set up cardboard box "hot dog" or "ice-cream stands" (with your child as the vendor to serve refreshments). Party guests can enjoy games of indoor balloon volleyball (pass a balloon over a string tied between two chairs), "sand"-castle-building (using pails, shovels, and uncooked rice or small noodles contained in a dishpan), and perhaps even beach blanket bingo.

Your guests might be tempted to take a break from all the excitement and lie in the sun; after all, why wait until summertime to catch some rays?

Giant Signs

Required:

Poster board, cardboard, art supplies, double-stick tape or nontoxic glue

Your children probably enjoy reading road signs when your family is traveling. How about getting them to create signs for inside your house?

Provide sheets of poster board or shirt cardboard, on which your kids will draw signs with markers or crayons. They can also draw the signs on sheets of colored paper, then affix the paper to the cardboard with glue or tape. Suggest starting off with simple signs like STOP, which can be used where a hallway enters a busy room. Your kids can also modify real signs: NO PARKING may become NO SLEEPING when placed over the sofa.

Encourage the creation of nonsense signs as well. How about WATCH FOR FALLING BANANAS or CAUTION: DINOSAUR CROSSING? Maybe your family needs a SPEED LIMIT: 2 MPH sign in the hallway leading to the playroom or a NO SNACKING ZONE warning on the refrigerator. Next time your children are running inside, you can pull them over and say, "Hey, didn't you see the speed-limit sign back there?"

Fun and Games

Gimme Shelter

Required:

Couch, blankets or large towels, chairs, blocks, red and orange paper, pot

Optional:

Flashlight

Imagine This

What better cure for cabin fever than having your child build his or her own cabin using the couch and some blankets?

For basic couch cabin construction, have your child stand the cushions on end, leaning against the front of the couch. Adding a blanket for a roof makes the rustic home ready for occupancy. If a bigger cabin for two or more kids is needed, have the troop use chairs as "poles" for hanging blankets or large towels. Also, a couple of small tables set side by side with a blanket or beach towel draped over them make a wonderful tunnel-like entrance that can lead to the "main living area."

Once the shelter is ready, details can be added to the homestead. A circle of blocks with a few sheets of crumpled red and orange paper make an ideal campfire. Larger blocks can serve as rock seats. Suggest using a floor lamp or table leg to tether a weary steed.

If the couch house is big enough for you, you might find that there are lots of advantages to living simply.

Godzilla Returns (Again)

Here's a winning activity for sci-fi fans that involves creating a monster right in your living room. Try these production and prop tips and ideas to get started:

Required:

Video camera, paper bags and toilet paper tubes, art supplies, cardboard boxes, newspapers, paper plate, couch cushion, table, sheet

- Paper-bag space helmets are easy to make; tape on toilet paper tubes to create a high-tech look. The monster can wear a decorated paper-bag mask.
- Couch cushions arranged in a tunnel make great caves for beasts to emerge from.
- For low-budget special effects, pause the camera, have all the actors freeze in place, then have the monster join the scene (appearing out of thin air) before restarting the camera.
- A cityscape can be created out of empty boxes, which will collapse dramatically when the monster stomps on them.
- A paper plate covered with aluminum foil makes a great flying saucer.

Recommend experimenting with different story ideas: For example, a scary visitor from another planet may turn out to be a good buddy after obvious (and amusing) language difficulties are overcome and fears are put aside.

Lights, Camera, Action!

Good Old Days Book

Required:

Writing supplies, art supplies, stapler, binder or report cover

How would your child like to read a story or history book that features you (or another relative)?

First, tell your child about an incident from your past (real or imaginary): perhaps a trip you took, meeting a new friend, or your wedding day. Then ask your child to write the story in his or her own words and illustrate the tale (a younger child might draw pictures, instead of writing text, to relate the story).

Alternatively, you can tell your child where you were when a famous historical event occurred (the inauguration of a president, an earthquake, and the like). Your child can then write and illustrate the historical tale as seen from your point of view.

You might suggest that your child include additional characters (your siblings, parents, childhood friends, and so on) and pictures of the clothes and hairstyles you wore. When the book is completed, you'll have just as much fun reading it as your child. Those *were* the days. . . .

Create-a-Book

Great Gestures

Here's a terrific way for a group of younger cabin-bound kids to vent some energy and have fun at the same time.

Have the children form a circle (without holding hands) so everyone can see all other participants. Then have the first person make a physical gesture and sound (perhaps your child can wave his or her right hand and say "Hello"). The person standing on his or her right repeats the action and sound, then the next person, and so on, until everyone is doing the same thing and making the same sound.

The first person then begins making a different gesture and sound, and one by one, everyone else in the circle switches to the new action and sound.

Alternatively, you can begin the game in the same way but have the first person stop after making a gesture and sound. The second person then repeats what the first did and adds an action and sound of his or her own. Continue until somebody can't remember the sequence or everyone's too tired to play any longer.

Fun and Games

Great Readings

Required:

Books, simple props and costumes

Reading aloud and storytelling are wonderful ways to entertain cabin-bound kids.

Dramatizing or embellishing a story doesn't have to be very complicated. You can, for example, have some simple props on hand to set in front of your child at appropriate points in the story. That way, when Max gets into his boat and sails away, your child can be holding a toy boat and sailing it across an imaginary ocean. Stuffed animals make especially good props.

For added pizazz, try including simple sound effects and costumes in your delivery. A simple costume for you or your child can add a new dimension to stories. You can also change hats to show different characters in the story. In addition, simply changing your position by standing, walking around, or getting down on the floor to show the action will often bring a story to life for your young audience.

Who knows, with a little practice you may be up for an Oscar for Best Storytime by a Mommy or Daddy!

Performances

Greatest Hits

If you and your child have a tape recorder, you can produce your own version of the *Greatest Hits of the Nineties*.

First, make a list of the tunes you want to record. Decide whether each song will be a solo, duet, etc., and write the name(s) of the performer(s) next to the title.

You might want to record songs based on certain themes (for instance, holiday songs, popular music, or old-time favorites), one topic per cassette. Or you and your child can compose your own songs. Choose familiar tunes and create new lyrics about your family, current events, or anything that strikes your fancy.

After you and your fellow performers have rehearsed the tunes, begin the recording session. You might not make the Top 40, but in your house at least the tape will be Number One!

Required:

Writing supplies, tape recorder

Sound Works

Group Authors

Required:

Paper bags

Optional:

Writing supplies, tape recorder, video camera

What happens when a group of cabin-bound kids work on a story together? Perhaps a great tale emerges.

Each child goes to a different room in the house and collects a bagful of items: a toy, a book, a shoe, a hat, etc. (You can specify the number of items to be collected.) One child retrieves an item from his or her bag and starts off a story. Perhaps the item is a doll: "Michele decided not to go to school today because . . ." The next person pulls an item from his or her bag and adds to the tale; if the object is a shoe, the sentence might continue: " . . . her shoes were too small." This process goes on until all the items have been incorporated into the story.

As an alternative, have family members select items for one another to add to the excitement and suspense. Look around the house and imagine the wild stories that would arise using common items as props, from soup ladles to handkerchiefs!

Try to capture the story sessions on paper, tape, or video; they're sure to be a family hit.

Imagine This

Guess That Sound

Shhh, what's that sound? You and your child will certainly enjoy finding out.

Close your eyes or turn your back and have your child find an item (either in the same room or another part of your home), then retrieve it. For younger children, you might want to preselect some unbreakable, kid-safe objects from which to choose. Your child then uses the item to make a sound, and you have to guess what the object is.

If you're stumped, ask for hints. For example, if your child is tapping the floor with your brown boots, he or she might say, "This is a sound that people sometimes make when they're walking." And if you need another clue, your child can add, "But you'd only hear this when it's snowing." Still haven't guessed it? Your child might then elaborate, "This came from your shoebox, and it matches your new jacket." Aha, you finally guessed it!

Then it's your child's turn: You choose an object and have your child guess what the sound is. For something that might sound really alien to him or her, how about the sound of running water (as in brushing teeth)?

Required:
Common household items

Fun and Games

Guess Where It Is

Required:

World atlas, paper and pencil for tracing

I f you have an atlas of the world, a pencil, and paper, then you have all you need to get a child or two through the Cabin Fever Blues. Try these geo quizzes with your geo whizzes:

- City Roster: Pick a state or country, then read off cities, starting with the most obscure and progressing to the most well known. How quickly can your kids figure out the state or country?
- Border Crossings: Choose a state or country, then see who, on the basis of bordering states or countries, can determine the place in question.
- Orientation Games (USA): List states that are north, south, east, and west of (but not bordering) the selected state, then ask who can figure out the mystery state.
- Guess-It-by-Shape: Trace a state or country and show the outline to the quiz show contenders. Can any of the players correctly identify your choice?

Fun and Games

Encourage your kids to make up their own intriguing questions. You'll be surprised at the minutia you learn. Quick: What state is home to Ashtabula?

Guess Who

This guessing game is fun for older children, especially in a group. It's a simple "Who am I thinking of?" game, with an interesting twist in how questions are asked and answered.

To start, have one player think of a person, either someone in the group or someone familiar to everybody. Then, all the other participants try to figure out who the subject is by asking questions to get clues. The questions must all be in the form of "If this person was a *blank*, what type of *blank* would he or she be?" What gets filled in for "blank" are common nouns, like *tree, car, song,* or an article of clothing.

In answering the questions, the first player has to try to think of some characteristic of the subject that compares to a particular type of tree, car, song, etc. For example, if the subject is very strong, he or she might be described as an oak tree. Or a tall subject could be a redwood tree. The players should keep asking questions until someone figures out the subject.

Now, if this person was a kid's activity, what sort of activity would he or she be?

Fun and Games

Hallway Pinball

Required:

Toilet paper tubes, cardboard boxes, ball

Optional:

Crayons or markers, construction paper, books

Here's a way to turn your hallway into a high-action sports arena.

Make a "tunnel" out of empty boxes and toilet paper tubes standing on end, wide enough to accommodate a rubber ball. The goal is to roll the ball through the tunnel without knocking over any of the boxes or tubes or getting stuck.

For hotshot pinball players, decrease the tunnel width or use a larger ball that's more likely to collide with the boxes and tubes. You can also make the game more challenging by setting books in the tunnel at angles, which will deflect the course of the ball.

For added fun, your child can decorate the boxes and tubes with construction paper or crayons and markers. You can also place toys in the path; perhaps the idea of the game is to knock over the alligator or deep-sea diver at the end of the tunnel. Encourage your kids to invent their own rules, the zanier the better.

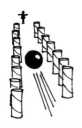

Hat Potato

Here's a neat takeoff on "hot potato" that's fun for younger kids.

To begin the game, each child needs a hat. Next, make up ten to fifteen "Hat Potato slips": small pieces of paper with simple but silly instructions written on them, such as "Hop on one foot and quack like a duck" or "Slither like a snake." Tape the slips to the outside of one of the hats (or write the instructions on stick-on notes and affix them to the designated hat). Then get a tape player ready with a selection of lively music.

Have the children sit sideways in a circle on the floor so that each child faces the back of the person's head in front of him or her. Each child also wears a hat. Once the kids are in place, turn on the music; have them remove their hats and place them on the heads of the children in front of them. This hat passing continues until you stop the music; whoever has the special hat takes one slip of paper from it and follows the directions on it (you or an older sibling can help prereaders).

Start the music, and pass the hat for this fun circle game!

Required:

Play or real hats, writing supplies, tape player, or radio

Optional:

Stick-on notes

Fun and Games

Hat Trimming

Required:

Hat, clear
adhesive
covering, art
supplies,
magazines and
other picture
sources,
recycled
materials

In the children's book *Jenny's Hat* by Ezra Jack Keats, a child is feeling bad about her plain old hat. But her bird friends come to the rescue with decorations such as a valentine, flowers, and even a bird's nest.

Even if your child doesn't have fine-feathered friends, he or she can construct a great hat. Take a strip of clear adhesive covering and wrap it around the top of your child's favorite hat, sticky side out. You might have to hold the covering paper in place with double-stick tape.

Now your child can festoon his or her hat by placing the following types of decorations on the adhesive covering: cutouts of flowers, people, animals, cars, geometric shapes; pictures from magazines, postcards, and junk mail; cotton balls; and anything else that will make for lively headgear.

With a hat like this, your child is sure to turn some heads.

Arts & Crafts

Historical Letters

Have you and your child always wanted to find out more about a historical figure such as Benjamin Franklin? Then why not suggest that your child write this person a letter? (You can even write a reply, in character, after the letter is "mailed.")

Required:
Writing supplies

Help your child think of some questions to ask the famous person: What was it like to live in your time period? What were the greatest challenges of your work? What were your most important accomplishments? What advice would you give to a young person who wanted to get into your line of work? How do you want people to remember you?

When your child has written some questions, he or she can add another paragraph or two describing what's happened in the intervening years. Wouldn't Ben be thrilled to hear about some of the gadgets we've invented since he discovered electricity, like the electric can opener and electric tie rack?

Great Correspondence

Required:

Writing supplies, stapler, binder or report cover

When was fire invented? And when did the first wheel turn? These are both questions that your child can answer in his or her own book of history.

The idea here is to let your child write a book detailing the history of the world from the earliest times to the present. First have your child create a time line showing the earliest date he or she believes we know of and continuing into modern times.

Next, suggest that your child write up key events (famous discoveries, inventions, battles, treaties, etc.), noting who was involved, a summary of what happened and when, and how the event changed the world.

Don't worry if the chronology or descriptions are correct; you can later suggest that your child do a little research for "additional" information about an entry in the book. The main goal is to have fun. Speaking of which, we were sure glad to learn that the radio was just becoming popular when the woolly mammoth was going extinct so that no one had to listen to traffic reports about pachyderm congestion on the expressways!

Create-a-Book

Is there a story behind the furnishings in your home? Have your child tell the tales.

Choose a piece of furniture such as a chair and let your child relate some imaginary stories associated with it. For instance, he or she might explain how this was the first chair ever used for seating purposes by a human being and how the cave people who invented it made various mistakes until they got it right (two legs just didn't cut it). Or perhaps the chair was originally owned by a famous Italian duke, Luigi XXXVI, who sat in it only while he played Frisbee with his hunting dogs.

Of course, you might want to relate some great real tales, too (like how your child laughed for the very first time while he or she sat in the chair and you made funny noises, or how a relative sat on a Popsicle that a younger sibling had put there for safekeeping).

Continue with other pieces of furniture in your house; everything, you'll find, will have its own unusual story to tell.

Fun and Games

Holidays from the Twilight Zone

Required:

Magazines and other picture sources, writing supplies, binder

Would your child like to have more days off from school for national holidays? Here's his or her chance.

This antidote for the Cabin Fever Blues involves inventing zany holidays for the nation or even the whole world to celebrate. To help your child brainstorm, provide a stack of newspapers, junk mail, mail-order catalogs, magazines, and other photo sources. Perhaps your child is fascinated with the idea of National Fruit Juicer and Vegetable Steamer Day. Or Stamp Out Plaque Week.

Younger kids can simply talk about the holiday; older children (who can also serve as "scribes" for siblings) can create a holiday "report," complete with the picture that inspired the event, when it is supposed to take place, how long it lasts, a description of the festivities, what people are expected to wear, who should observe the event, songs to be sung, and so on.

Place the write-ups in a three-ring binder and you've got a complete holiday planner. How will *your* family be celebrating National Tree Frog Day?

Imagine This

Home Helper

87

▶Adult Supervision

Required:

Large cardboard boxes, markers, oatmeal container, cardboard tubes, container tops, brads, empty food boxes, craft paper

Did you ever wish your kids could help you out during the day with cleaning and other chores? Well, here's an opportunity to get your young children involved in the magic cleanup routine that takes place while they're in day care, school, or bed.

Use cardboard boxes to create some appliances, say, a washer and a dryer. Cut out a lid (your job), then trace container tops for dials. You can also affix container tops with brads (available in any stationery store). Tape the projections of the brads on the inside to protect fingers. Perhaps provide some small boxes of detergent and the like (empty food boxes covered in craft paper) and some "laundry" in need of cleaning.

While the wash is going, your child might want to help vacuum. An oatmeal container makes a fine vacuum canister, and a paper towel tube, cut halfway through at one-inch intervals, makes for a good hose, which can be affixed to the oatmeal container. A toilet paper tube cut in half lengthwise can be used for the "attachment."

Hey, isn't this great? But what will *you* do while your helper takes care of the housework?

Fun and Games

Home Sweet Home

Required:

Notebook and paper

Optional:

Tape measure or ruler

So you think you know the fine details of your house, apartment, or condo? After you do this activity with your child, you'll know the real nitty-gritty of your home.

If your child knows how to use a ruler or tape measure, have him or her jot down all the vital measurements: the dimensions of each room, the size of door frames and windows, the distance between the kitchen and the front door, and so on. Kids who don't know how to use measuring tools can simply pace off the rooms or devise an arbitrary standard, such as the bronto (the length of a particular toy brontosaurus from head to tail).

Next, have your child do vital counts: light switches, electrical outlets, doorknobs, light fixtures, and other household essentials that you probably don't have a handle on yourself.

Capture all this information in a notebook; it might prove invaluable the next time you need your home appraised.

Fun and Games

Homemade Art-Supply Organizer

Does your child have a tough time keeping all of his or her art supplies neat and accessible? Then suggest making an organizer box to sort things out.

First supply a shoebox or similar-sized carton; your child can cover it with white or craft paper, then decorate it with a personal flair. Next, have your child sort out what he or she wants to store in the box (that will determine the size and shape of the required sections).

The dividers are made from strips of thin cardboard, such as the type that dry cleaners use to package shirts. Each strip should be cut a bit longer than the space it needs to span so there's enough at the ends for your child to fold back and glue. Small cardboard gift boxes or check boxes can also be used to create divided sections. Toilet paper tubes, which make excellent paintbrush holders, can be trimmed and glued in the organizer as well. Small items like paper clips and rubber bands can be placed in envelopes that can be stored in the box.

When the organizer is done, your child will have a place to store all the supplies that went into making it.

Required:

Shoebox or carton, thin cardboard, toilet paper tubes, nontoxic glue, scissors, craft or white paper, art supplies, envelopes, small gift boxes or check boxes

Arts & Crafts

Homemade Piggy Banks

Required:

Egg carton, small boxes, milk carton, cardboard tubes, kraft or construction paper, art supplies, tape and nontoxic glue

Why does a piggy bank have to look like a pig? It doesn't. Here are some alternate banks you can make at home.

Frog Bank. Supply your kids with a small box (such as a pound sugar box). Have them cover it with green construction paper. Lay the box flat. Your child can now cut out four legs from the construction paper and glue them onto the sides and front. Now, remove two compartments from an egg carton for your child to first paint green, then glue onto the top near one end of the box. Cut a slot in front of the eyes to receive coins. Your child can then use a marker to incorporate the slot into a big happy smile that says, "Feed me!"

Mailbox Bank. Have your kids start with an empty milk carton taped shut at the top, with a flap cut in the slanted portion. Glue half circles of cardboard at the tops of the sides, then add a third piece of cardboard curving partway over the circles to form the top. They can finish it by covering it with blue and red paper.

As your kids will learn, there's nothing like the feeling of money in the piggy bank.

Arts & Crafts

House Hunting Challenge

Do your kids really know what's in your house? They probably think so, but these hunting challenges will get them to take a closer look.

To play, simply have your children find different items in your house that fall in certain categories or have particular characteristics. Here are a few to start with:

Color matching. Have your kids pick something at random, then find ten items in the house that are the same color.

Double duty. How many items can your children locate that have more than one purpose, such as a step-stool/chair?

Two by two. Send your children through the house to find everything that comes in pairs, like shoes, bookends, socks, or closet door handles.

Majority rules. What single item in your house outnumbers all others? The answer can be practical (light switches) or silly (pieces of yarn in your carpet).

Opposites. Have your children find one pair of opposites (big/small, heavy/light, high/low) in every room.

On with the hunt!

Fun and Games

How does a chicken cross the room?
No, it isn't a new riddle; it's animal
charades!

Family members take turns traversing a
long hall (or the perimeter of a room that's
been cleared of breakable objects) while
role-playing an animal. A person pretend-
ing to be a kangaroo might hop (stopping
occasionally to check on the baby kangaroo in her pouch), a leopard-lookalike
might take giant leaps, a giraffe-actor
might crane his or her neck to drink, an
elephant-player might tread heavily (while
munching peanuts with his or her trunk),
and so on.

After the actor takes a walk (crawl,
hop, etc.), other players take turns guessing what the creature is; if nobody figures
it out, the actor crosses the room again,
this time offering verbal clues as well. The
person who guesses correctly gets to play-
act the next animal.

You can limit the animal possibilities to
certain categories, and establish a nonver-
bal sign for each one (say, flapping arms to
indicate a bird). Of course, you can also invent a sign for the toughest animal-charades
category of all: imaginary creatures.

Fun and Games

Impromptu Performances

This activity can help take the edge off cabin fever by giving everyone a chance to "get their sillies out."

On three-by-five-inch index cards, write various antics that your kids can perform. Organize the actions by categories, such as Animal Impersonations ("Roar like a lion") or Acts of Dexterity ("Hold a ball in your open hand and hop around the room two times").

Have your kids decorate the backs of the cards with crayons or markers. Encourage them to keep the categories consistent so that all blue cards will be Animal Impersonations, all red cards will be Acts of Dexterity, and so on.

Next, place a large piece of paper on the floor. Use crayons or markers to draw a "target." Color in each ring of the target, making sure all of the colors of your cards are represented on the target. Place the cards near the throwing line, organized in color-matched stacks. Each player tosses a rolled-up pair of socks onto the target, picks a card the same color as the circle that his or her sock landed in, then follows the instructions.

Sound silly? Then you've got it!

Required:

Pencil and index cards, large sheet of paper, art supplies, socks

Performances

In Your Child's Own Words

Required:

Tape recorder

Wouldn't you like to hear what you thought and did when you were young, in your own words and your own voice? Well, you can't go back in time, but you can help your child record his or her feelings and experiences on tape and create a treasure that will be appreciated for many years.

To begin, have your child tell you about some important events in his or her life in the past week or month. Encourage him or her to include anything at all that comes to mind (your child may find it helpful if you go first by telling something about what you've been doing). Some topics to include are school experiences, activities with friends, visits with relatives, or family outings. Once your child is ready, set up a tape recorder with a blank tape so he or she can begin recording a diary on tape.

Who knows, these tapes may end up as part of a documentary when your child grows up to be a famous person.

Sound Works

Indoor Horseshoes

They say that "close only counts in horseshoes." Well, if you're close to your wit's end about what to do with your cabin-bound kids, this indoor horseshoe game may be just the thing.

Make six horseshoes (three for each player) by cutting U-shaped pieces about six inches long out of corrugated cardboard. To add weight and strength, layer three cutout pieces, insert several pennies between them, then tape them together.

For the target, cut four one-inch-long slits in the end of a paper towel tube to form tabs, fold the tabs out, and tape them to a one-foot-square cardboard base so the tube stands up straight. Place a book or other object on the base to keep it from falling over during the game.

Establish a throwing line and pass out the horseshoes. A horseshoe that lands around the stake is called a "ringer" and is worth two points; the horseshoe that lands closest to the stake earns a point. Of course, your children can make up their own scoring system from scratch.

Ah, if we could only make a pony to go along with these horseshoes . . .

Required:

Sheets of corrugated cardboard, paper towel tube, tape, pennies, book or heavy object

Indoor Sports

Indoor Olympics

▶Adult Supervision

Suggested:

String, onion-bag balls (see 168), wrapping paper tube

The Olympics, the pinnacle of sports achievement, right in your living room! You can stage your own indoor Olympics by putting together an assortment of simple sports challenges for your cabin-bound kids. To get your children into the spirit of the games, have them put together their own Olympic uniforms (T-shirts, pj's, sweats, etc.) and start off with these indoor sporting events:

Slither race. Contestants slither along the length of the room on their stomachs, without using their arms or hands.

Balance beam. Athletes walk on a piece of string on the floor.

Weight lifting. Tie two onion-bag balls (activity 168) to a wrapping paper tube for a pretend weight-lifting competition.

Triathlon. Combine three simple activities for a triathlon event.

Knee races. Have the competitors kneel on the rug for this race.

Indoor Sports

Signal the start of the games with a shout from a toilet paper kazoo and watch the athletes strut their stuff!

Indoor Park

How would your young child like to be a park ranger? All you need is a nearby park (or a home that you can turn into one).

First, you'll need a "landscape artist" or two (your child and other family members can volunteer) to design the grounds. Have them "plant" trees, shrubs, and gardens (by hanging homemade posters on the wall as backdrops or creating building-block foliage. They can also arrange "natural" sculptures (made from modeling clay or Play-Doh) and animals (stuffed teddy bears, bunnies, and so on).

Next, have your child/ranger act as guide and show "visitors" around the park. Make sure that he or she points out all the major attractions, and have the tourists take turns asking questions about the flora and fauna.

The ranger and tourists might also engage in a discussion about park-related issues: fire prevention, wildlife protection, recycling trash, etc. After all, you'll want to keep your park safe, friendly, and clean for future visitors.

Suggested:

Large pieces of paper, art supplies, building blocks, clay or Play-Doh, plastic bowl and milk jug, stuffed animals

Imagine This

Indoor Treasure Hunts

Required:
Writing supplies

Optional:
Cookie or treat

Even Sherlock Holmes had to start somewhere en route to becoming a great detective. Here's how to get your child started on the road to finding clues that lead to great treasures.

As in the traditional treasure hunt, the idea is to place clues around the house, with the first clue leading your child to the second, the second to the third, and so on until he or she reaches the treasure (a cookie or appropriate treat, perhaps).

The twist here is to rename the rooms of the house and devise appropriate clues. For instance, the kitchen might be named the North Pole, and a clue leading to the refrigerator might read, "Find the paper stuck to the giant iceberg of the North Pole." Younger children can join in the fun by having older kids read and interpret the clues.

Play this a sufficient number of times and you might just launch your child's professional detective career.

Fun and Games

In-House Weather Reporter

There's no need today to dial the weather number for a forecast; simply ask your resident expert for a report.

Have your child draw a weather map (by outlining the country, adding some major cities and states, and filling in details such as rain clouds, sunshine, and temperatures). Your child's map can be realistic and based on a recent forecast, or it can be a product of wishful thinking (say, a reading of ninety degrees when it's actually snowing). Try spicing up the map with unusual symbols, like cats and dogs for a heavy downpour.

Your child can refer to the map while delivering the weather forecast to you, pointing to various places and giving the current weather conditions (you might also want to combine this with a taping or video activity such as 112 or 131).

In any case, you'll probably be glad that it's safe to leave the house without your umbrella, despite those ominous clouds.

Required:
Map of the United States, art supplies, large sheet of paper

Optional:
Tape recorder or video camera

Performances

In-Print Hunt (Older Kids)

Required:

Books, magazines, and other print sources

This version of In-Print Hunt will appeal to children with reading skills. Have your kids locate specific items (or items in a specific category) in dictionaries, encyclopedias, books, and magazines. They're all grist for the find-it mill. Try these categories or invent your own:

Geography. Have your kids find selected names of cities and countries.

Human-made. How many pictures of human-made objects can your children find? Locate one picture for every letter of the alphabet.

Animal kingdom. Your children can try to find names of selected animals and sort them into different classes (mammals, reptiles, birds, fish, amphibians).

Names. Have your kids count common names, such as "Robert" or "Bob."

Finally, what about sending your book explorers on an expedition to find the most unusually named critters on the earth? Perhaps someone will stumble onto a picture of Australia's very own rabbit-eared bandicoot.

Fun and Games

In-Print Hunt (Younger Kids)

Here's a "find it" game that will keep your prereaders poring through books, magazines, and newspapers in search of items that you specify for them to locate. Use these categories for starters:

Required:
Books, magazines, and other print sources

Things That Move. Have them look for pictures of trains, boats, cars, trucks, airplanes, bicycles, skates, and so on.

Animals. Keep the animal picture hunt simple for younger kids by having them find big animals and small animals.

Colors. First have your children point to, say, all the green things, followed by all the red things, etc.

Different Parts of the House. How many pictures of kitchens, bedrooms, bathrooms, and the like can your kids find?

Shapes. See how many round things your children can find, then square things, and so on.

Finally, how about locating happy faces, which we hope you'll see when your kids do this activity!

Fun and Games

Instant Vacation

Required:

Art supplies

Optional:

Writing supplies, ring binder, tape recorder

Oh no, another cabin-bound day! With the help of your child, you can be somewhere else warmer or sunnier, at least in your mind's eye.

Ask your child for suggestions about places that he or she thinks would be great escapes from the snow or rain (perhaps the beach that you visited last summer or some other vacation spot). Then break out the art supplies and set your child to work illustrating a "winter vacation," including transportation, lodgings, dining possibilities, activities, and so on.

An older child can caption or write a brief story about each picture or act as a scribe for a younger sibling. You can also tape the tales for a "talking book." Or place the pictures in a ring binder and have your child tell the tale behind each scene.

Nothing beats the real stroll down a sunny beach, but a fireside chat with your winter vacation book is still a great reprieve from a cabin-bound day.

Create-a-Book

Intergalactic Gala

If there's a planet that your child hasn't
had a chance to visit yet, why not have
him or her book some space there for
your next gala party?

Have your child choose the planet, real
or imagined, and make the "reservations."
Your child can then organize the packing
of appropriate clothing as well as party
food and drink. Depending on the atmos-
phere of the planet, you might want to
fashion space helmets (paper bags with a
cutout in the front).

When the preparation is done, you and
your child, along with other cabin-bound
kids, can climb aboard a spacecraft (chairs
lined up in a row) for a ride to the stars.
Be sure to take turns describing the celes-
tial sights: planets, comets, and everything
else you pass on the voyage. Once you ar-
rive, have your party-goers check out the
environment, do "anti-grav" gymnastics,
search for friendly life forms, comment on
the view of earth, and so on. Then break
out the supplies for a "touchdown" meal.

Whatever you do, this party is sure to
be out of this world.

Required:

Party fixings,
large paper
bags

Celebrations

It's Great to Be . . .

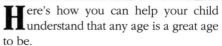

Required:

Writing supplies, stapler

Here's how you can help your child understand that any age is a great age to be.

Give your child three or four sheets of paper, a pencil, and verbal instructions to write his or her current age at the top of the first page. On subsequent pages, your child can write some of the important ages he or she has been (a ten-year-old might have pages entitled "ten," "six," "two," and "newborn").

Then ask your child to make a list of all the best things about being each of those ages. He or she can include abilities, privileges, events, hopes and ambitions, and so on. For example, on the "newborn" page, your child might list: "Met my family," "Learned new things all the time," etc. Under "two," he or she might write: "Learned to run," "Made my first friends," "Visited Grandma," and so on.

When your child is finished writing, staple the pages together and put them in a safe place. He or she can add to it periodically upon discovering the best things about being an older kid

Fun and Games

Junior Autobiography

Who says that only important grown-ups can write their life stories? Your child can chronicle his or her early days anytime.

Have your child compile a book about his or her past. You can provide details about the birth, homecoming from the hospital, infancy, learning to walk, etc. Your child can add his or her own memories (first day of school, learning to read, making a best friend, and so on).

Alternatively, your child can create a fictional book in which the main character is him- or herself as a toddler. Other characters might include junior versions of family members and friends with, say, twenty years deducted from all the grown-ups' ages.

Your child will undoubtedly want to include pictures of all the characters. He or she can take advantage of the opportunity to draw a self-portrait, or perhaps you can donate a baby picture or two.

Required:

Writing supplies, stapler, binder or report cover

Optional:

Baby pictures

Create-a-Book

▶Adult Supervision

Required:

Washable stamp pad or pencil, paper, tape (not necessary if you use a stamp pad), cornstarch, small soft brush

Optional:

Magnifying glass

This activity will amaze your child and possibly reveal who's had his or her hands in the cookie jar.

First explain that everyone has unique fingerprints. Then have your child print everyone in the house today. You can either use a washable stamp pad or rub a pencil on a piece of paper to make a sheet of graphite. Show your child how to hold a finger and gently roll it onto the stamp pad or graphite back and forth, then place the finger on a piece of paper, again rolling it once from one side to the other. This will leave a clear fingerprint (if you use graphite, put clear tape over the print to keep it from smudging). Label the prints with each person's name.

Next, dust various objects with cornstarch and a small soft brush (you'll get the best prints off hard and smooth surfaces). Blow off the powder and *voilà!* You'll see the fingerprint of whoever has touched the object. Try matching up fingerprints with fingers (a magnifying glass will help).

Now fess up, aren't those *your* prints on the cookie jar?

Fun and Games

Junior Soothsayer

Even if you don't have Chinese food tonight, you can enjoy fortune cookies.

Have your child write out custom fortunes for each member of the family and place them in envelopes, empty film canisters, or other small containers. Your child can also help you set the table and place loose fortunes under family members' placemats or plates. The fortunes might focus on topics such as:

Required:
Writing supplies, envelopes, film canisters and other containers

Upcoming events. "You will ace your history test."

Household events. "It will be sunny for our picnic on Sunday."

Fanciful thinking. "A great tornado will straighten up your room tomorrow."

Hopeful thinking. "Mom will bake your favorite cookies today."

Very hopeful thinking. "Dad will lose his new low-fat, low-salt, no-sugar cookbook."

So, what does the soothsayer believe your prospects are for getting through the day without an attack of cabin fever?

Fun and Games

Required:
Writing supplies

When was the last time you read an easy-to-follow instruction manual? Perhaps you can encourage your child to write a how-to booklet in simple, straightforward language that anyone, even a grown-up, can understand.

Have your child choose a favorite assembly project, such as constructing a house from blocks or Legos. He or she can then write or type precise instructions (a younger child can explain it verbally while you capture the directions on paper). Your child can also refer the reader to step-by-step illustrations ("see figure 1," etc.).

Another how-to pamphlet possibility is a routine multistep task or chore (tying a shoe, setting a table, brushing teeth, and so on).

Once your child has completed the manual, see whether you can follow the instructions to the letter. If the text or pictures get confusing, ask the writer to revise them for you. Wow! Imagine a custom-made manual that even comes with customer service!

Fun and Games

Kid of All Trades

If your child is handy with tools, perhaps he or she would like to open up a hardware store right at home.

Have your child gather the inventory and arrange the items by category: paper towel tubes and toy rings (for the hardware department), cardboard and poster board (for lumber), straws and milk jugs (for the plumbing area), and so on.

Then, become your child's first customer. Walk into the store, describe a mechanical "problem" that you're having around the house, and see whether your child has the gadget and the know-how to solve it.

And while you're at it, you might want to have your child duplicate some keys, repair a broken appliance, or explain how to begin a home improvement project (and sell you the supplies you'll need to complete it).

Maybe a combination wall-smoother/floor-leveler is just what you need to refinish your basement. . . .

Required:

Paper towel tubes, cardboard and poster board, straws, milk jugs, toy rings

Main Street

Kids' Guide to the Galaxy

Required:

Writing supplies, art supplies, stapler, binder or report cover

Where does fire go when it goes out? Where does the sun go when it sets? Why do grown-ups stop growing even though they keep eating? What's the ozone hole and why don't we just stuff a big cork in it?

You can find out the answers to these and other cosmic questions when your children write a book of the universe based on *their* knowledge base. Each entry can consist of a few sentences or paragraphs and can be accompanied by an original drawing that helps explain the topic.

To help your child write an entry, ask questions in a variety of subject areas: astronomy ("Where does the sky end?"); biology ("What if dinosaurs were alive today?"); botany ("Can plants feel?"); or geography ("How do we know that the earth is round?").

With any luck you'll learn the answer to one of the most perplexing problems of humankind: What happens to socks that disappear in the laundry?

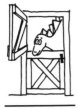

Create-a-Book

Latest Fashions

Would you and your child like to participate in a very unusual fashion show? Here's your chance.

Have your child collect his or her favorite or silly ensembles, making sure he or she includes a variety of clothes (casual, formal, sportswear, etc.). (For an offbeat show, you might also want to adapt some of the wacky outfits in Fashion Show of the Absurd, #59.)

Then have your child dress in the first outfit and glide down the "runway" (the perimeter of a room, a hallway, etc.) while you videotape him or her. You can add the narration: "Here comes Michele wearing a floor-length flannel nightgown set off by the latest in elbow pads, waterproof mittens, and a designer ski cap." Then put the camera on pause while your model changes outfits. Have your child "hit the mark" again and roll tape.

If your child is also a capable videographer, you might want to model a line of adult fashions for the camera yourself. Isn't it gratifying to know that both you and your child have such chic taste in clothes?

Required:

Video camera, clothes

Lights, Camera, Action!

Local Video News

Required:
Video camera

Optional:
Poster board,
art supplies

We interrupt this playtime to bring you a special report. All the kids in the neighborhood got together for a baseball game Saturday, but the game was rained out and both teams retreated to Timmy Smith's house for chocolate chip cookies.

From your child's perspective, there are scads of newsworthy events happening right in your own neighborhood. What better way to capture the fun than with an all-kids local news show. Have your child write and produce a show featuring *really* local news: important events like who lost a tooth, who has a new baby sister, or more strange reports from the haunted house around the corner.

You might want to do the filming while your child sits at the "anchor desk" (your dining room table, perhaps with a poster-board background decorated to look like a skyline). For added fun, suggest that your child stop for a commercial (see activity 134) now and then to break up the news.

In addition to being fun, this activity may start your junior newshounds on a career in network broadcasts. Get ready, CNN!

Lights, Camera, Action!

Long Distance Pals

If you've always wanted to have a pen pal, then why not establish a correspondence with your child?

Before you begin, you and your child can invent characters for yourselves complete with names and histories. Also, decide where your characters live (another city, state, country, or continent).

Now, have your child write (or type) you a letter in character. The first letter should introduce the pen pal and tell about his or her family, an ordinary day at school or work, what the weather is like, unusual events that have taken place recently, favorite household activities and games, food preferences, etc.

When your pen pal is finished, he or she can fold the letter and "mail" it to you (perhaps have a younger sibling help decorate a cardboard mailbox for the occasion). After you've read the letter, send back a reply that introduces your own character. Remember to include some thoughtful questions; you'll want to ensure that your new pen pal writes back soon.

Required:
Writing supplies

Optional:
Cardboard box, art supplies

Great Correspondence

Look through Any Window

Required:

Pencil and paper and/or art supplies

Even when you're cabin-bound, the world outside is constantly changing.

Here's an activity your child can begin in the morning, continue at intervals (say, every hour) throughout the day, and finish at dinnertime. Have him or her look out the window (the same window each time) and write a paragraph or draw a picture about what he or she sees *at that moment*. Emphasize changing or moving items (clouds, cars and trucks, pets, etc.). During each "window-watching" session, your child can update his or her notes or draw a new picture.

You can have your own "parallel" window-watching sessions. Accompany your child to the window every hour or so and write descriptions or draw "photos" of what *you* see. At the end of the day (or activity), compare your vision of what's out the window with your child's. Discuss the changes each of you saw. Not only is it likely you noticed some different things, but it's also possible that you and your child have entirely separate views of the very same neighborhood.

Fun and Games

Made to Order

If you and your child could create a mail-order business, what would you sell?

Required:

Magazines, junk mail, and other photo sources, double-stick tape or nontoxic glue, scissors, writing supplies, stapler, binder or report cover

Cull items from magazines, advertising circulars, junk mail, and catalogs to get some ideas for products you'd like to carry in your own catalog. Be open-minded; consider everything from office supplies and electronic gadgets to toys and gourmet foods.

Have your child glue or tape the pictures onto pieces of paper (say, three to a page). He or she can then create copy for each item. (An older child can use a word processor or typewriter; a younger child might dictate the text to you). Your child can also include a price for each item. (A four-million-dollar tennis racket, anyone?) To complete the catalog, have your child create an order form (clip one from another catalog as a sample). Place the pages in a binder or report cover, or staple the pages together.

The catalog will not only be great fun to make, but the next time you're stuck for a gift idea, you'll know just where to look.

Create-a-Book

Magical Moms and Dads

Required:
Piece of cloth

A silly magic show can be a great way to entertain a bedridden child or cheer up a grumpy kid on a cabin-bound day. Here are a few silly stunts to get you started:

Empty head. Put your index finger in your ear and your tongue in your opposite cheek; it will look like your finger is in your cheek. Move your tongue as you move your finger.

Thumb trick. Hold your hands together with the tip of your left thumb replacing the bent-down tip of your right thumb and your left forefinger hiding the junction of your two thumbs. When you hold your hands at the correct angle and separate them slightly, it will appear to your kids as if you're taking off the top of your thumb.

Magic ring fingers. Form a circle with your thumb and forefinger on each hand. Ask your child to assist by covering your hands with a piece of cloth. Hook the circles together, say "Abracadabra," and have your child pull the cloth away. *Tadaa!*

Fun and Games

Now, if you could only make all those dishes disappear . . .

Magical Mystery Machine

As this activity will prove, imagination is the real mother of invention.

Gather up an assortment of art supplies, odds and ends, lids, spools, foil, and shoeboxes and have your child build an imaginary machine (one that turns spinach into ice cream, sounds an alarm when baby brother enters the room, or polishes the cat's claws). Your child can start with a plain shoebox and add plastic lids and paper arrows for dials, cardboard tubes for feeding in "raw material," and yarn for "drive belts." Encourage the inventor to decide on a purpose for every piece he or she puts on the machine. Suggest decorating the devices with tempera paint, markers, recycled foil, and pictures cut out of magazines, junk mail, catalogs, and so on.

Later, say after dinner, have your child make a presentation to the rest of the family, explaining in detail what the gadget does and how it works. (This will be great to catch on videotape, if you can).

Just one question: Does the cat get to pick which color claw polish she wants?

Required:

Boxes, recycled household materials, magazines and other photo sources, art supplies, tape and nontoxic glue

Optional:

Video camera

Imagine This

Make a Speech

Required:

Writing
supplies, bag

Do you have a great topic for a speech? Then share it with your children and listen to the idea develop.

Have each person select several topics (to jump-start the process, you might designate a theme such as geography, history, careers, or sports). Each child should write down the ideas on slips of paper and put them into a bag.

Now have your first speaker choose a topic from the bag. Give him or her a few moments to silently "rehearse." The actual speech should last as long as the speaker is inspired to talk.

A variation of this activity is to have participants choose objects (toys, drawings, books, and so on) but keep them out of sight. Then, just before speech-making time, someone gives the speaker an item. This can present quite a challenge; have you ever tried to make an extemporaneous speech about a cheese grater?

Performances

Make an Ad

Are you and your child tired of seeing the same old newspaper and magazine ads? Here's how to take revenge on the advertising pros.

Browse through newspapers and magazines, then clip photos as well as bits and pieces of copy from ads, reassembling them into wacky hybrids that parody or spoof the originals. Add a wild headline (the more incongruous the better), then affix all the pieces with glue or double-stick tape to a sheet of paper or poster board.

When you and your child have finished your "ad campaigns," pass the ads back and forth or take turns reading the headlines and text aloud, seeing who can suppress their giggles the longest. If a group of cabin-bound kids are playing, each participant can stand up and do a dramatic reading of his or her ad.

Twenty percent off the price of ear polish that three out of four city senators recommend? Sounds great to us. . . .

Required:

Magazines, newspapers, and other photo and text sources, double-stick tape or nontoxic glue, paper or poster board, scissors

Photo Fun

Map Makers

Required:

Writing supplies, art supplies

If your child is fascinated by maps, this activity will beat a path to fun and learning.

Start with an area most familiar to your child: the backyard or the area surrounding your house or apartment. Suggest that he or she draw landmarks such as a garage, steps, a fence, garden, sandbox, etc. Also suggest drawing the compass directions, but don't worry about the accuracy of the map; the idea is simply to allow your child to express his or her understanding of local geography.

Once the backyard is drawn, expand the map or start a new sheet so that it covers a block or two and includes the streets and their names, the houses of neighbors and friends, stores, traffic lights, stop signs, and any noteworthy landscape features your child can recall.

Then see if he or she can chart the entire town in which you live, perhaps even expanding to the state and including various cities. Again, don't fret about accuracy; this mapping activity is measured in units of F-U-N.

Fun and Games

Marble Painting

Here's a new twist (or more accurately, shake, rattle, and roll) on painting that your child is sure to enjoy.

▶Adult Supervision

Required:

Cardboard box, marbles or Ping-Pong balls, tempera paint, paper, masking tape

Provide a large box, then have your child place a piece of paper inside. If the box is significantly larger than the paper, tape down the edges with masking tape. Next, give your child a handful of marbles (supervise carefully if young children will be participating in the activity; Ping-Pong balls may be more appropriate). Your child covers the marbles with tempera paint, then places them on the paper in the box. As he or she shakes the box, the marbles will create interesting swirls and patterns.

Encourage experimentation: Perhaps your child might introduce one marble at a time or place the marbles in the four corners of the box before beginning the shaking action.

As your child gets more comfortable controlling the roll of the marbles, he or she can try to create specific patterns. For the ultimate challenge, see if your child can write his or her name in "marblelese."

Arts & Crafts

Meet Myself

Required:

Writing supplies

Here's something that a world-class journalist like your child rarely gets to do: write about him- or herself!

Have your child write a Q & A column that includes answers to some of the following questions:

- When and where were you born?
- Who are the other members of your family?
- Can you describe the neighborhood where you live?
- What are your favorite games and activities?
- What things make you happy?
- What do you want to be when you grow up?
- Which of your accomplishments and achievements make you the proudest?
- What would you say is the biggest problem the world faces today? How do you think we could solve it?
- What are your plans for the future?

Fun and Games

After your child writes (or types) the piece, he or she can give it a title (perhaps "The Life Story of the Kid at 25 Mill Street"). And don't forget, your child should also give him- or herself a byline.

Memory Tester

This game is a combination of follow-the-leader and Concentration that will make paying attention *fun* for a group of cabin-bound kids.

Gather the players in a spot with a good view of one or more rooms in the house, pick a person to start, and have everyone watch carefully as he or she walks to an object and touches it before returning to the group. Then, have the next player repeat the actions of the first child and add a second item to the selection by touching it. Each child in turn repeats the steps of the previous one and adds something else.

You can challenge the group to try and remember, say, ten items or have the players limit their selections to particular types of objects, such as things you sit on. You can also have them do something more complicated than just touching an item; they could, for instance, pick up a book or magazine and read one sentence out of it.

Uh-oh, it's your turn, the magazine just blew shut, you can't remember which plant Sam touched, and the cat is leaving the room.

Fun and Games

Micro Explorers

Required:

Magnifying glass (preferably with a plastic lens), large bag, art supplies, pencil and notebook or pad

Optional:

Tape recorder

Imagine This

A magnifying glass can be your child's springboard to creative explorations and great yarns. Here's how to structure an adventure into the world in miniature, right in your living room.

First select a "site" for your child's indoor "field trip" (say, the living room couch), then send him or her off with an explorer's bag (knapsack, tote bag, or shopping bag) that contains a magnifying glass with a plastic lens, writing and art supplies for sketching the unseen realms. For prewriters, a tape recorder can be a good way to capture the details of perilous journeys. Encourage your child to report on textures, patterns, and various surface features not visible to the naked eye.

When your child returns from the journey, suggest making up a story based on what he or she saw. Perhaps there's a miniature dinosaur civilization living in the grains of wood in your floor, or a world populated with a miniature family (yours). Or a world with a Cheshire cat and a mad hatter who throws tea parties. . . . Wouldn't *that* make for a great story line?

How would you like to have a roomful of imaginary creatures created by you and your child?

Pantomime a creature (a bird, fish, insect, animal, etc.), then ask your child to invent a name for the creature and tell you where it lives, what it looks like, what it eats, how it travels, etc. Your child can create a sound for the animal to make (purring, bleating, barking, and so on) and vocalize it while you portray the animal.

When you and your child have developed the creature's "character," have your child suggest a situation (say, building a home for the winter or looking for a playmate) that the two of you can improvise together (you pantomime while your child makes the sounds and narrates the story).

When the scene ends, trade jobs: Have your child mime a creature while you invent an animal background and language. How many creatures can you and your child create in an hour?

Mix-and-Match Storybook Characters

Required:

Books, thin cardboard, art supplies, nontoxic glue or double-stick tape, pencils, straws or chopsticks

Can you fathom a tea party attended by Captain Hook, Alice in Wonderland, Winnie the Pooh, and Pippi Longstocking? You can host such an event right in your own playroom puppet theater.

Trace characters from your child's favorite storybook onto pieces of thin paper, then affix the paper to sheets of cardboard with double-stick tape or glue. Cut out the characters and have your child decorate them with crayons or markers. Finally, affix the backs of the finished characters with tape to unsharpened pencils, straws, or chopsticks. You're now ready for a little mix-and-match storybook puppet action: Nobody could make Captain Hook mind his manners better than Pippi, and Alice is sure to find all the honey that Pooh could ever want.

As a variation, trace people from history books, as well as animals, dinosaurs, or mythical beasts. What do you suppose George Washington would have done when his men encountered a relative of the Loch Ness monster while crossing the Delaware?

Imagine This

Money in the Bank

▶Adult Supervision

Required:
Cardboard boxes, egg carton, writing supplies, chain or string, junk mail

Who needs automatic teller machines when you can have a bank right at home and set your own hours?

Have your child set up a "teller's window" with deposit and withdrawal slips (cut-up junk mail or pieces of used paper), a pen on a chain (or string), a computer terminal (made from boxes), and a cash register (an egg carton), etc. Supply some coins, too (supervise closely if toddlers will be joining the play).

See whether your younger child can help you with some simple transactions (like accepting money for a deposit or cashing a check). Your older child might assist you with more complicated banking matters (counting change, exchanging your money for foreign currency, issuing traveler's checks, and so on).

Then, trade places. You become the teller and your child can take on the role of the customer. Your child might just learn a valuable lesson while he or she is banking: Money really doesn't grow in egg cartons.

Main Street

Mystery Story

Required:

Tape recorder

Can you and your child coauthor a great story knowing only a minimum of what the other is plotting? Find out with this cabin-fever-busting activity.

Set up a workspace (if possible, choose a room with a door) and arrange a tape recorder on the table. Have your child leave the room, then record the title and the first couple of lines of your story. When you reach a "cliffhanger" (an exciting spot in the narrative or simply the word "and"), hit the stop button and ask your child to come back into the room. Tell him or her the last five words of your recording, then leave the room. Your child then records a couple of lines to the story and tells you his or her last five words as you switch roles. Continue in this fashion until the story reaches a conclusion.

When the narrative is complete, play back the tape with the two of you in the room. You're bound to get a few chuckles as the tale takes some strange twists and turns.

Sound Works

Neighborhood Story

Is there anything interesting happening in your community? Then have your child write a book about it.

Your child can write a true story about some of the people, buildings, and issues in your neighborhood: a new ice cream store, a new kid on the block, an unusual insect or "archaeological" find, and so on.

Or your child can invent a tale about some things that probably *haven't* happened in your neighborhood: the day the president came to town, the time when all of the pets on the block drove the car to the park, etc. Your child can even combine fiction and nonfiction by featuring real-life people such as family members and neighbors in the story.

If your child is a history buff, he or she might want to write a book about your neighborhood's early days: who the first settlers were, where they lived, how they dressed, and so on. Your child can even create a whole new background for your neighborhood straight out of his or her imagination—like the "fact" that your block was actually founded by the crew of the *Mayflower*!

Required:

Writing supplies, stapler, binder or report cover

Create-a-Book

130 New Year's Eve

Required:

Toilet paper tubes, newspapers, streamers, balloons and other decoration materials

Why wait until December to enjoy New Year's Eve when you and your child can celebrate it anytime?

First, create "noisemakers" (toilet paper tubes) and party hats (using old newspapers). Then, transform your home with garlands/chains, streamers, banners, balloons, and confetti. Set the clock forward and count down the minutes and seconds.

Next, list some yearlong resolutions. (You can either reaffirm the goals you set last December or establish new ones). Then, you and your child can take turns offering advice for sticking to your plans. Be sure to establish some short-term resolutions—the sillier the better. For example, you and your child might resolve not to say the word "I" for the rest of the day. Do you think you can keep it up until the clock strikes twelve?

Celebrations

News Radio

You're tuned to radio station WBZR, where the weather is always bizarre and the news is always unbelievable. Have your child use a tape recorder to create nutty news, silly sportscasts, and wacky weather reports. To get your child's imagination rolling, read these samples:

Required:
Tape recorder

"Smallville was rocked today by the news that Miller's Pond is being overrun by giant blue catfish. The local game warden has come up with a plan to introduce even bigger orange dogfish to control the situation. No word yet on availability of giant dogcatcher fish in any color."

"At the World Standing-on-One-Foot Championships today there was an upset when Michael Smith lost his balance after only ten minutes. Jennifer Long was disqualified early on in the competition due to illegal nose-twitching."

Encourage your child to embellish his or her radio personalities with silly voices and funny names. "Reporting for WGFY, this is Billy Banana. Now back to Sarah Spaghetti in the newsroom."

Sound Works

132 Nightlife

Required:

Writing supplies, stapler, binder or report cover

What *really* happens while the family sleeps? Ask your child to "publish" a book about his or her nighttime visions.

Your child can write a fanciful story about all the things that the household furniture and appliances do while he or she is asleep (for instance, the table might stretch its legs, the teakettle might whistle show tunes, and the telephone might call a friend). Your child might also incorporate other nonhuman characters, such as those gremlins who hide things when we're not looking.

Alternatively, your child might want to take a more serious tack and write about some of the things that actually happen while he or she sleeps (such as adults staying up late to finish household chores, nocturnal animals foraging for food, and people in other parts of the world getting ready to start the day).

This book, when finished, will undoubtedly make a very interesting bedtime story.

Create-a-Book

No "Ors," "Ands," (or) "Buts"

Want to hear a great story? Then create one with your child, a word at a time. (As you'll see, this is also a neat activity to do with a word processor.)

Required:
Writing supplies

Optional:
Word processor

Have your child say or write any word to begin the tale. Then you add a word, and your child adds another, until the first sentence is finished. This cooperative writing approach continues until the story comes to a conclusion. It may or may not be the ending you had envisioned, but that's the whole point: You never know what direction the tale will take when you and your child become coauthors.

Once you've gotten the hang of cowriting a story in this fashion, up the ante by introducing a new rule: No one can use the words "or," "and," or "but." That's a lot more difficult than it sounds. Take turns inventing new rules, too, just to keep each other on your toes.

Gee, that's going to be tough when you can only use words less than five letters long. . . .

Fun and Games

Now a Word from Our Sponsor

Required:
Writing supplies, video camera

Optional:
Poster board

H as your child learned to view commercials with a critical eye? Perhaps making one of his or her own will provide some insights into the world of advertising.

Before taping, your child should write a script for a familiar product, keeping in mind who the commercial is for and what qualities of the product he or she wants to feature. The script might include descriptions of the product as well as "scientific studies" your child has conducted on its usefulness. Most important, it should include a tag line or jingle.

Once the script is done, your child can display the product in a well-lit room and create a set for the commercial by moving around couch pillows or making backgrounds on large pieces of poster board. If a demo is desired, you might be called in to do the filming while he or she touts its virtues.

When the commercial is finished, sit down for a private viewing. Be warned, though, you just might be motivated to rush out to your local store and buy the featured item or gizmo.

Lights, Camera, Action!

Obstacle Course Bowling

This combination of bowling and pinball is as much fun to build as it is to play.

Required:

Soft rubber balls, blocks, boxes or books, cardboard tubes

All you need are some soft rubber balls (those used in racquetball are ideal), blocks, boxes, or books for obstacles, and cardboard tubes for targets. Have your children build the obstacle course so that a rolled ball can bounce off the obstacles and ricochet toward the target. If your designers/engineers build the course in a narrow hallway, they can include the walls in their design. Have them experiment with different angles and combinations of walls, and include narrow passages or tunnels that the balls must pass through.

Encourage older children to make a more complicated course. They could, for example, build a series of target blockades and make each one a little harder by adding more obstacles.

Keep your eye on the ball, you never know where it will go. . . .

Indoor Sports

Opinion Game

Required:

Writing supplies

How do your child's opinions match up with yours and vice versa? Here's a fun way of finding out.

Create a survey with ten multiple-choice questions. For instance, "The best toy in the house is *(a)* the wooden building blocks, *(b)* the kids' stove, or *(c)* the train set." Or, "My favorite weather conditions are *(a)* snow, *(b)* fifty-five to seventy degrees, or *(c)* a steamy hot beach day."

Write the opinion poll on one sheet of paper. Then, on a separate sheet of paper, write down what you believe will be your child's answers. (Make sure your child doesn't see the answer sheet.) Now read the survey questions to your child and see how many times you correctly predicted his or her answer.

Let your child compose an opinion poll next and see whether he or she can match your answers. So how would your child say you would answer the following question: Being cabin-bound is *(a)* an opportunity to try new things, *(b)* usually pretty exciting, or *(c)* all of the above?

Fun and Games

Organization Kids

Does your playroom or child's bedroom look as though a tornado hit it? Here's how to find some emergency relief and prevent future disasters.

Required:

Cardboard boxes, craft paper, art supplies, magazines and other photo sources

Gather cardboard boxes of various shapes and sizes. Have your child cover them with craft paper (lids should be covered separately). Decorations can include photographs from magazines and junk-mail catalogues (perhaps you can even find and use photos of the toys themselves) or freehand crayon or paint designs.

Have your child decide which box will contain which type of toy (perhaps the largest box will contain giant stuffed animals, medium-sized boxes will hold building blocks or large dinosaurs, and the smallest boxes will hold Legos, marbles, etc.). Have your child label each box with its contents and his or her name.

Then make a game of having your child put the toys into their new places: For example, challenge your child to fill a box in five minutes or do the two-foot toy toss, which entails tossing soft toys into their bins from two feet away. Quick, put the lids on before the toys can escape!

Arts & Crafts

Our Old House

▶Adult Supervision

Required:
Video camera, play or real tools

There's always an audience for a video-tape about home repair, and your child might be just the person to narrate this sure bet.

Have your child gather his or her "tools" (store-bought or homemade toys). Then have him or her undertake a make-believe home-improvement project (fixing a leaky faucet, repairing a broken chair leg, installing new cabinets, and so on) while you work the video camera.

Next have your child rehearse his or her demonstration. "Roll tape" while your child explains to the audience, step by step, everything that he or she is doing to get the job done. Suggest that the on-screen mechanic also describe each piece of equipment as he or she uses it and tell the range of tasks for which it is useful.

Finally, your child can offer special hints that will help viewers when they attempt their own repairs. Just think of all the money you could have saved on home maintenance if you'd had this tape to guide you along!

Lights, Camera, Action!

Oversized Homemade Checkers

Why settle for conventionally sized checkers when your kids can create a giant checker set that's as fun to make as it is to play with?

To start, gather twenty-four paper plates or plastic lids and have your children decorate them so that they have two sets of twelve "checkers" each. (If you use plastic lids, you'll probably need to glue on circles of paper to make decorating easier.) Have the kids decorate the bottoms of the playing pieces with a distinctive design (like a crown or face) so that a piece can be flipped over to show that it is a "king."

Next, have your children cut sixty-four squares of paper (thirty-two each of two colors) slightly larger than the playing pieces; you might need to draw cutting lines for them. They should then place the squares on the floor in an eight-by-eight-square grid with colors alternating and tape the edges together as they go.

Now clear your room; you're dealing with major-league games!

Required:

Paper plates or plastic lids, regular tape, double-stick tape or nontoxic glue, art supplies

Fun and Games

Paper Bag Helmets

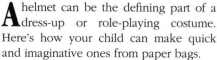

Required:

Paper bags, art supplies, recycled materials

A helmet can be the defining part of a dress-up or role-playing costume. Here's how your child can make quick and imaginative ones from paper bags.

To begin, gather up a variety of paper bags, as well as markers, scissors, scraps of cloth and paper, cardboard tubes, and other decorative add-ons. Prepare each bag for your child to decorate by folding the top down three or four times to form a one-inch rim. Then cut out part of the bag to expose some or all of your child's facial features: You can make eye or nose holes, a single "viewing band," or an opening for the entire face.

When the cutting is done, have your child use markers to transform it into a particular type of helmet (football, space, motorcycle, whatever). Suggest gluing cardboard tubes on the sides for lights or space thrusters and making similar use of other recycled materials as well. Your child can even cover the helmet with scraps of fabric to turn it into a bird head-dress.

If your child uses his or her noggin, there's no limit to the kinds of helmets that will come out of your headgear factory.

Arts & Crafts

Party Blower
Target Shoot

We've all played with noisemakers that unfurl a paper tube when you blow through them. Here's how to use them to chase away the Cabin Fever Blues.

Required:

Party noisemakers, toilet paper tubes, dominoes, small boxes

Gather up some lightweight targets and one party blower for each player. Toilet paper tubes, dominoes, empty single-serving raisin boxes all make great targets.

For a warm-up game, line up five to ten targets on a table and have each player knock them over one at a time with the party blower.

Now try randomly arranging numbered targets on the table and see if your children can knock them down in order. Or place a row of targets down the middle of a table and have two players try to knock them down from opposite sides.

Yet another variation is to have your children play "party-blower hockey" using a Ping-Pong ball for a puck, with opposing teams trying to score goals by knocking the ball off the opponents' side of the table. One nice feature of this game: Every goal automatically includes a noisemaker celebration!

Fun and Games

Personal Memento Museum

142

What does your child cherish the most? You'll find out when you visit his or her personal memento museum on this cabin-fevered day.

First, designate a room to be used as a museum. Then, ask your child to select some of his or her favorite possessions (photos, drawings, toys, school projects, etc.). An older child might want to include awards, certificates, and trophies that he or she has won. The "curator" can divide his or her museum into "exhibit sections," with each devoted to a different theme (school, hobbies, and so on).

Have your child make a placard for each display (with a title and a brief description) and then prepare a script for a guided tour. As a museum-goer, you can ask questions about the displays or swap stories with the tour guide.

Who knows, maybe you'll finally learn the significance of that gum wrapper your child has been saving all these years. . . .

Imagine This

Pet Interview

What's on Rover or Tabby's mind? Your child can find out with this activity.

Have your child write out or tape an interview with the family pet (if you don't have a pet, an imaginary one will do). You can also jot down the answers while your child speaks for the critter in an authentic voice. Suggest various questions for your child to ask and your pet to answer, such as:

Required:
Writing supplies

Optional:
Tape recorder

- What's the best part about being an animal?
- What's your favorite human food?
- What is it about humans that bothers you the most?
- If you could be a human, what kind of job would you want to have?
- Would you want to change places and have a person as a pet?

Suggest that your child also interview animals that he or she has seen in books, such as extinct or exotic species. Be sure to place the write-ups in a notebook.

So your cat thinks humans are untrainable; wait till she sees you practicing your new backflip!

Imagine This

Pharmacy Fun

Required:

Writing and art supplies, double-stick tape or nontoxic glue, ice-cream-making and serving supplies, art supplies, real or make-believe pharmaceutical items

When was the last time you enjoyed an old-fashioned soda at a drugstore counter? Here's a chance to show your child a glimpse of the past.

Help your child arrange some goods (cosmetics, make-believe medical supplies, small toys, etc.) in your at-home "pharmacy." He or she can make signs for each "aisle," attach price tags for each item, and hang notices of special sales ("Snowstorm Clearance Sale, 25 Percent Off All Purple Items," etc.) on the wall.

You can help your child set up a "soda counter," complete with ice cream, toppings, fruit, milk, and sparkling water. You'll also need some glasses, spoons, placemats, and a menu.

After you've shopped for a while, have your child wait on you at the soda counter. Perhaps he or she can sell you on the soda of the day or offer proven recommendations for easing cold symptoms, sore feet, or tired ear lobes.

Main Street

Phoney Phone Book

W|ho needs another phone book when those we already own are tilting the shelves. This version won't weigh in at such an inconvenient tonnage and will certainly be much more interesting.

First, create "residential" entries. Have your child make a list of people's names. Include silly monikers (such as Larry Lego or Billy Blocks), storybook characters, or famous people. Then ask your child to create an address and a phone number to match the name.

Older kids will especially enjoy creating the yellow pages for imaginary businesses. Help your child think of oddball companies, such as Pencil Stubs to Go (whose job is to recycle pencil stubs by selling them to people who prefer them over new pencils). For each, your child can create a logo and some text, including an address and phone number.

You can also have your child create entries for each of your family members and friends as well. So how does it feel to have your name published in a book with some of the world's most famous people?

▶Adult Supervision

Required:
Writing and art supplies, stapler, binder or report cover

Create-a-Book

146 Picture Postcards

Required:

Writing and art supplies, index cards, magazines or other photo sources, nontoxic glue

Do your children love getting postcards from friends and relatives traveling in exciting and exotic places? Have them create their own postcards to mail from an imaginary journey.

Supply your children with five-by-seven-inch index cards for the blank postcards and have them add pictures to the front and greetings on the back. They can draw original pictures or glue on photos cut from magazines to depict their imaginary travel destinations, complete with descriptions and notes about their activities. Have them finish their postcards by adding pretend postage stamps.

You can also have your children make a mailbox to mail their postcards from (the role of mail carrier would be an excellent one for a younger child to play). Older children can actually mail their postcards; make sure that addresses are legible and that all glued-on pieces are secure first.

Having a wonderful time, wish you were here!

Arts & Crafts

Picture This . . .

147

Here's a drawing game that's sure to delight your kids and test your ability to describe the world about you.

Think of an object, say, a house, a building, or a car. Then describe it to your child in terms of geometrical shapes and see if he or she can draw what you had in mind.

For instance, you might describe a house with three windows and a door as follows: "Draw a square and place a triangle on top of it. Now place a rectangle inside the square, with the short side facing up. Place three smaller rectangles inside the square as well." You might be very surprised at the final result. But even if it doesn't look like a house, that's OK; the idea of the game is to have fun and stimulate your child's imagination to name the resulting drawing. Switch roles and see how you do with your child's description.

An alternative way to play the game is to call out random shapes, with no particular final object in mind, and see what turns up on the paper or chalkboard.

Maybe this is how some great modern artists got started. . . .

Required:

Art supplies or chalkboard and chalk

Arts & Crafts

Ping-Pong Ball Target Bounce

Required:

Ping-Pong balls, paper bags, tall plastic cups, empty frozen-juice containers, shoeboxes

Kids love the way Ping-Pong balls sound when they bounce them. Why not add some simple targets and give them something to shoot for?

Paper bags, tall plastic cups, empty frozen-juice containers, and shoeboxes all make great kid-safe targets. (Stuffing paper towels in the bottom of the targets will help keep the balls from escaping.) Your kids can shoot for a single target at a time, for multiple targets in a line, or for targets randomly scattered around a room.

They can also try to get the Ping-Pong balls into the targets in a single bounce, or they can specify the number of bounces each throw must take. And they can make the game more challenging by trying to bounce the balls over obstacles like a wall of blocks or a piece of string tied between two chairs. For younger children, make the targets larger and have them simply toss the Ping-Pong balls into them.

Want a really silly game? Change the targets to things like one of Dad's shoes, a cup of water, or a cereal bowl (skip the milk).

Indoor Sports

Plot Swap

How would your child like to reshape a classic tale?

Have your child choose a story, then discuss the plot with him or her (who were the main characters, how did the story start and end, what was the turning point, what lessons were learned, etc.). Talk to your child about how you might improve (or just change) the story.

Perhaps you can add new characters, change the names of the old characters, or place the story in a new setting. You might change antagonists into heroes or have characters solve their problems without quarreling or using magic. And you can also change elements of the plot. For example, maybe Cinderella, the daughter of doting farmers, is able to go to the country fair through the kindness of her aunt; at the fair she wins top honors for her pumpkin pie à la glass slipper!

Then ask your child to retell the tale, incorporating all of the changes. So how's that for a wild yarn?

Imagine This

Poster Art

Required:

Art and writing supplies, large paper or poster board

Posters are art with a message. Perhaps your children have a cause to support or event to commemorate. Have them design and create posters that will put *their* message on the wall to share with the whole family.

Here are some topics that they can illustrate with big, simple pictures and lots of color (it helps to sketch a layout first in pencil):

Family Publicity. Have your children make a poster to announce an upcoming event like a holiday dinner or family picnic.

It Happened Here. Have them commemorate an event like a big snowstorm or the latest case of chicken pox in their class.

Arts & Crafts

Family Public Service Announcement. Your children can make a poster to support some family project or goal, such as proper use of the recycling bin or conserving water.

Hey, maybe with the right promotion on the fridge, your kids will actually start eating more broccoli.

Presidential Pen Pal

151

How would your child like to have a pen pal who works in the Oval Office?

Have your child write a letter to the "president" (you). Your child might ask the president questions or offer opinions about real or imaginary issues of the day, then "mail" the letter (in the family cardboard mailbox). After you've read the epistle, write an appropriate reply.

Now reverse roles. You write a letter to your child, the newly elected president. Pose questions about world affairs, community issues, etc., then have your child answer your letter with one of his or her own.

Once you've received a letter from the president, you can exchange another round of letters or switch roles with your child and begin again. Either way, you'll want to encourage your child to keep up a letter exchange between your home and the "White House." You just might be the first to learn that our nation's currency will soon be printed with bright purple ink and feature the heads of famous dinosaurs.

Required:

Writing supplies

Optional:

Cardboard box, art supplies

Great Correspondence

Required:

Magazines and newspapers, double-stick tape and nontoxic glue, scissors, Popsicle sticks or plastic spoons

Here's an activity that will prove puppets are not only entertaining but also newsworthy!

Collect a pile of old newspapers and magazines. With your child's help (and a safety scissors, if appropriate), clip out photographs of familiar people (elected officials, actors, sports celebrities, and so on). Then glue the pictures onto cardboard, trim around each person, then tape them to Popsicle sticks or plastic spoons to make puppets.

You and your child can choose a favorite tale (or create a tale of your own) and "cast" the saga (decide which pictured person is appropriate to play each role).

Whatever the roles, you and your child can have the selected puppets perform the story onstage (the edge of a tabletop), ad-libbing the lines as the two of you go along. After all, real characters deserve to deliver true-to-life dialogue.

Photo Fun

Quick Mimes

Can your child convey a wealth of meaning through physical gestures alone? Have him or her pantomime some of the following (without props):

- Walking, feeding, and playing with a pet dog
- Getting dressed, brushing teeth and hair, and leaving for school
- Unwrapping birthday presents and blowing out the candles on a cake
- Picking flowers and arranging them in a vase
- Cooking dinner, setting the table, and serving the meal
- Playing a game of tennis, baseball, soccer, etc.
- Collecting shells at the seashore, taking a dip in the ocean, and building sand castles

Your child can also choose his or her own actions to mime, and you can guess what he or she is doing. Of course, you can try some mimes yourself. How does it feel to ride an invisible covered wagon over the Continental Divide?

Performances

Quote of the Day Holder

Required:

Large envelope, scissors, art and writing supplies, newspapers, books and other print sources

Here's an easy art project that can lead to an ongoing fun and educational family activity: a framed holder for posting tidbits and trivia. Your child can use it to display a "quote of the day," "word of the day," or notes from "this day in history."

The frame itself is simple to make. Cut a rectangle out of the front side of a large envelope, leaving a one-inch border all the way around, and have your child decorate it, including a title for the selected category. Next, punch a hole through the front end and the flap so nothing will fall out when it's hung up. Each new quote, word, or other interesting tidbit can be written on a clean piece of paper and put in the envelope so it shows through the frame.

Your child can look for quotes in the newspaper or in favorite books, encyclopedias, and dictionaries; for variety he or she can make up original quotes, silly words, or historical nonevents.

Say, this *is* fun; you can quote us on that.

Arts & Crafts

Railway Travelers

You and your younger child can turn your home into a major transportation center to anywhere.

Have your child set up a ticket counter (a table with some homemade tickets), a baggage-check area nearby, vending machines (a shoebox filled with bags of treats), and other train-station items.

Then, of course, you'll need a train. Help your child set up a row of chairs, with a special seat (and a control panel made of cardboard, yogurt container tops, etc.) for the engineer. Your child can put on a special engineer's hat before he or she gets behind the wheel.

The engineer can discuss the scenery and landmarks during the trip. You might also talk about some of the things you'll see and do once you reach your destination. You could visit the food car or take in a meal with the engineer during a scheduled stop: Traveling sure works up a hearty appetite!

Required:

Table, shoebox, treats, cardboard, yogurt container tops, play hat, writing supplies

Main Street

Rainbow Cubes

▶Adult Supervision

Required:

Ice-cube trays, food coloring, plastic container

Nothing brightens up a cabin-bound day like a rainbow. If none are handy, your child can make one in the comfort of your kitchen.

Fill an ice-cube tray *part*way with water (you don't want the water overflowing the individual compartments). Then, have your children add food coloring to the water; a drop per cube is plenty. Encourage your child to be adventurous and mix and blend the colors. (Remember that concentrated food coloring can stain furniture, so work on newspapers and break out the painting smocks.)

Place the tray back in the freezer and allow the water to freeze. Remove the frozen cubes and place them in a plastic bowl or dish for observation (not for use in drinks); as the cubes melt, the colors will stream and swirl, adding to the fun.

For a fancier frozen rainbow, your child can layer colored ice in a plastic container. Color about half an inch of water in the container at a time, allowing it to freeze before adding the next layer.

Whatever colors your child chooses, the rainbows are certain to brighten up the day.

Fun and Games

Reach Out and Touch Someone

Most young kids seem to be telephone freaks; not only are the buttons great fun to push, but the phone seems to be such an important part of grown-ups' lives. Here's a time-honored way to give your children a phone line of their own, without giving your local Bell a dime.

Take two clean yogurt containers (eight-ounce size) and punch a hole in the bottom of each one (your job). For a nice personal touch, your children might enjoy decorating the yogurt containers. Next, cut a string about ten feet long and thread it through the holes. Tie a knot inside both containers to keep the string from slipping out.

Operating the phone is simple. The message sender talks into one container while the recipient listens through the other. It's important to keep the string taut, or the sound vibrations won't be passed along between the two "phones."

Suggest that your child use the phone in various play situations (pharmacy, police station, business, and so on). Maybe even dial up the weather and find out when the sun will shine again.

Required:

Two empty yogurt containers, scissors, string

Optional:

Art supplies

Fun and Games

Read the Fine Print

Required:

Art supplies, scissors, double-stick tape

What's in a label? A prescription for curing a kid's Cabin Fever Blues.

The idea of this activity is to create labels for various food products in your pantry (canned foods, mixes, cereals, bottles of juice, and so on). Provide paper, pens, scissors, and double-stick tape.

Encourage your child to devise clever names and tag lines. A can of chicken soup might acquire the line "Great for a Morning Gargle," and the ingredients might include 100 percent natural mud and beach sand. Your child might rename a product altogether. A can of peaches might be relabeled "Golden Lotus Floor Wax—One Stomp to an Unbelievable Shine!"

A box of cake mix might include zany directions, such as: "Add mix to 3,500 gallons of apple juice; mix well with canoe paddles or ocean-liner propeller. Pour into small round pan. Bake for six years, cool for two years. Place under elephant for five minutes before serving."

You'll never read labels the same way after this activity.

Fun and Games

Recycled Art

Reduce, reuse, recycle . . . relief! Your children can join the "throw less away" movement, entertain themselves, and enjoy a fun project at the same time.

Required:

Recycled materials, art supplies, tape or nontoxic glue, toothpicks

Dig out your recyclables and have your children make the following kinds of truly original artwork:

Packing-peanut collage. Glue foam packing peanuts on paper to make a picture. For added pizazz, your children can color them with markers.

Tube frame. Notch the ends of four cardboard tubes (your job) so they can be taped together at right angles to make a picture frame, then decorate it.

Insect collection. Use foam peanuts for bodies and toothpicks for legs to make a fantasy insect collection.

Scrap faces. Glue castoffs onto light cardboard: film canister lids for eyes, foam peanuts for eyebrows, a section of an egg carton for a nose, and soft foam for lips.

What else can your kids come up with? There are limitless ways to recycle the artistic imagination.

Arts & Crafts

Rosetta Stones

Required:
Writing supplies

The Rosetta stone enabled eighteenth-century scholars to decipher the hiero-glyphics of ancient Egypt by providing "parallel" passages in Greek and Egyptian. You can invent your own Rosetta stones right in your living room, and you won't even need a hammer and chisel.

Take a piece of paper and list all the letters of the alphabet in a column. Next to each letter, place a different geometrical shape, arrow, simple picture, or other visual substitute.

Now write out a message using the "graphic alphabet," hand your child the translation sheet, and see if he or she can read the correct words.

And for a hotshot code buster, try this: Leave about three quarters of the letters as they are but substitute graphics and symbols for the rest. Write out a message in the "hybrid" alphabet and see if your child can crack the code *without* a translation sheet.

S✳! ℰL?✳S? ✳:Δ □\✳:K !0★

(Which means: Enjoy this activity!)

Fun and Games

Roving Radio Reporter

"Why?" and "What's that?" may be the most frequent phrases uttered by children. Wouldn't you like to turn that natural inquisitiveness into a fun activity?

Required:
Tape recorder

Here's a way to encourage your child to ask questions and *listen* to the answers. Have him or her make a newsradio–style tape recording with the following kinds of programming ideas:

News features. Your child can interview friends or family members about work, school, favorite pastimes, or hobbies.

Topic of the day. Have your child report on a particular topic like Mom's garden or an event in the news, such as an election or major sporting event.

Opinion poll. The "newscaster" can conduct a radio survey among friends and family members about a familiar local topic, such as "Which is the best playground in town?" or "Where can you buy the best ice-cream cones?"

Be sure to "tune in" when the tape is finished if you want to be an "informed" citizen.

Sound Works

162 Sales Call

Required:

Common household objects

What's your child selling? Why not schedule a sales call and find out?

Designate a place (a desk and two chairs would be ideal) and time for the sales call and make sure that your child dresses "professionally" for the occasion (after all, he or she will want to make a good impression). Then ask the salesperson to put his or her "wares" (whatever household objects are being "sold") on the table and give you the best sales pitch possible.

Be sure to examine the goods closely and ask questions that any "informed consumer" would surely pose. For instance, if your child is selling fruit, you might want to know, "Are these apples sure to keep the doctor away?," "Do you sell prepeeled bananas?," or "Is glow-in-the-dark watermelon also available?"

Your child can use his or her answers to point out additional virtues of the products: "Yes, we sell glow-in-the-dark watermelon, and it comes with a no-rind guarantee!"

Imagine This

Say It with Type

Typography plays such an important role in what we read: It conveys moods and tells us how important, how serious, or how casual is the written message. This activity will get your child thinking about type as more than a way to represent words.

Have your child write words in a style that conveys their meaning or feeling, such as the following:

STAND UP

LAY DOWN

AROUND THE WORLD

GETTING STRONGER

FEELING SHAKEY

Or how about this one:

BREAK OUT!

Arts & Crafts

Scrap Stamp Painting

Required:

Art supplies, recycled materials, small objects, toys

Do your kids love to paint? If so, here's a new way to apply their artistry.

All your children need to create some original artwork is tempera paint, paper, and a collection of found objects to use as stamps. Almost anything will do: film canisters, foam packing peanuts, erasers, crumpled paper, paper clips. They can even roll toy cars through the paint to make tire tracks or use plastic animals to make footprints.

Pour the paint into dishes or plastic lids wide enough for the objects selected and supply each of your children with a large sheet of paper. They can stick with abstract designs or take inspiration from the first shape they put on the paper to create their picture (a circle can become a head, a square or rectangle can be the start of a city, or a splotch from a piece of sponge can become a wave crashing on a beach). Your children can also use more conventional tools (brushes and fingers) to complete their paintings.

What to do when their masterpieces are done and dried? The kids can stage their very own art show in the playroom gallery.

Arts & Crafts

Sculpture Museum

Do you have any skilled sculptors in your home? If so, collect an artwork assortment and display it in an at-home "museum."

Your children can create and exhibit sculptures made from modeling clay, foam cups, pipe cleaners, sponges, playing cards, empty cardboard boxes, and cardboard tubes attached with tape or glue.

You can choose a theme for the pieces (animals, holidays, vacation places, etc.) or have your children simply create works of art as the mood strikes them. In any case, display your artists' masterpieces prominently on the kitchen or dining room table. Be sure to make up, with your child's help, cardboard placards that include the sculptors' names, the titles of the pieces, dates created, the "media," and any other information that will give viewers a better understanding of the artwork. Each child can take turns showing "visitors" the collection and explaining the fine points of the exhibit.

Who wouldn't be proud to act as curator of *this* museum?

Suggested:

Modeling clay, cardboard boxes and tubes, tape or nontoxic glue, playing cards, recycled materials, sponges, blocks, thin cardboard, markers

Imagine This

Sensational Salon

Required:

Large cardboard box, hair dryer and mirror (or make-believe equivalents), clips, ponytail holders, barrettes, headbands and other hair accessories

Feel like pampering yourself? Then pay a visit to your home beauty salon and let your child transform you into a model.

First, have your child furnish his or her beauty parlor with a real or pretend sink (a box), mirror, hair dryer, chairs, etc. Style supplies (clips, ponytail holders, barrettes, headbands, and so on), should also be stocked. Choose your treatment (new style, shampoo, coloring, or whatever); you and your child may find unusual hairstyles to duplicate in magazines or newspapers, or your child can work from your directions or pure imagination.

Of course, your child's beauty services might also extend to other areas, such as manicures, massages, facial masks, and makeup. In fact, why not ask for an entire makeover; with your child's skills, you'll surely be the talk of the town.

Main Street

Shoebox Topiary

Here's a cardboard menagerie where anything goes, whether it has six legs, three eyes, or blue fur.

To begin, assemble an assortment of shoeboxes, empty milk cartons, small cardboard boxes, and cardboard tubes. Have your children create realistic or fantasy animals, starting with a large box for the body and adding a smaller one for the head, with cardboard tubes for the legs and neck. (You can make the cardboard tubes easier for your children to attach by cutting a series of half-inch slits in the end and bending back the tabs for gluing.)

After your children have made the animals, they can attach bottle caps for eyes, shoelaces for tails, paper cups for ears, pieces of plastic straws for toes, or whatever strikes their fancy. They can also glue on shreds of paper for fur or, for a real topiary look, cover their creations with pieces of green paper for leaves.

When their animal creations are done, you can have your children make a table-top zoo. But please don't feed the animals!

Required:

Shoeboxes, empty milk cartons or small cardboard tubes, paper cups, recycled materials, string or shoelaces, nontoxic glue, art supplies, straws

Arts & Crafts

Shooting Hoops

Required:

Mesh onion bag, newspapers, rubber band or string, large paper bags, duct tape, masking tape, string

Indoor Sports

Here's a way to have some basketball fun in your living room. You don't need a ball and you don't need a basket; here's how to make your own.

For a ball, use a mesh onion bag filled with wadded-up newspaper and held closed with a rubber band or knotted string. Crumple the newspapers loosely so that they fill up the onion bag.

To make a basket, double up two large paper bags, fold the tops down two to three times in one-inch folds for stiffness, and cut the bottoms out. You may want to add a strip of duct tape around the top for added strength. Then attach the bag to the back of a chair, either with masking tape or string laced through small holes punched in the top strip, and you're ready to begin the game.

Have your children start by seeing how many baskets they can get in ten throws from a fixed line. As their shooting improves, you can have them try more challenging games like taking a step back after each successful shot they make. With a bit of practice and a change of weather, you'll be ready to take the Living Room Trotters for their debut in the major leagues.

Every household needs to have rules, including some just-for-fun ones.

Have your child help you establish a "constitution" of silly laws. You might include these or similar mandates: Everyone has to clap his or her hands three times before standing. Family members must walk around their chairs three times before and after each meal. Kids must take one giant step after saying the word "I."

You and your child can then organize the crazy rules into such categories as "mealtime rituals," "early morning silliness," "for rainy days only," and "before-bedtime buffoonery."

If you want to make the laws "official," have your child create a "Silly Laws" constitution. He or she can use tracing paper (to stand in for parchment) and write with a broad, felt-tipped pen (so that it looks like quill and ink). Finally, you'll want to have your child sign the document before displaying it on the wall; you might need to prove at some later time that you were authorized by a top official to jump up and down twice before brushing your teeth.

Required:

Writing supplies

Optional:

Tracing paper, broad felt-tipped pen

Fun and Games

Sing-a-Song Book

Required:

Writing supplies, stapler, binder or report cover

Are you and your child a musical duo? Then why not "publish" a book of your own compositions?

You can create a catchall songbook (including a variety of melody types) or one that has a specific kind of music (show tunes, ballads, holiday songs, and so on). If you and your child are old hats at writing music, then you might want to include "the best of" the tunes you've already written.

To create new songs (even if you can't read and write music), choose a familiar melody. With your child, you can create new lyrics. Remember to write the name of the original song at the top of the page so you can recall the melody later.

Alternatively, your child can copy notes from actual sheet music and write his or her own lyrics below. Or you and your child can create your own musical "language," inventing a staff, beats, rests, etc. You can even create your own mnemonic to help you remember your own unique notes: Every Gifted Composer Deserves Recognition.

Create-a-Book

Smart Solutions

Need some advice? Why not tap into your child's wisdom?

Write a letter to an "advice columnist" (your child) detailing an imaginary dilemma. For instance, you might ask what to do about a child who will eat only popcorn and whether or not it would be appropriate to speak in dinosaurese at a fancy dinner party or restaurant.

Have your child explain (by letter) how he or she would solve the problem: Perhaps the recommendation will be a slew of healthy popcorn dishes such as popcorn-adorned spaghetti, popcorn-flavored fruits and vegetables, and popcorn-infused casseroles. As for speaking dinosaurese, perhaps that should be restricted to meals that you eat with reptiles.

Once your problem has been solved, switch places: Have your child write a letter to your column. Then, respond with *your* best advice.

So, do parents really know best?

Required:

Writing supplies

Great Correspondence

Soft Croquet

Required:

Cardboard tubes, yardsticks, rubber bands, newspapers, paper, corrugated cardboard, foam balls, markers, masking tape

Here's a simple way to enjoy croquet indoors.

First, make croquet mallets by attaching toilet paper tubes to the end of wrapping paper tubes or yardsticks with rubber bands. Stuff the toilet paper tubes with newspapers and tape the ends.

To make the wickets, fold a sheet of paper lengthwise several times to form a long narrow strip, then make a right-angle fold across each end of the strip. Next, bend the strip into an arch and secure it to a sheet of corrugated cardboard by taping down the folded ends. A traditional croquet course consists of seven wickets laid out in a figure eight, with an additional wicket above and below the top of the 8. But set them up as you wish.

Use foam balls for the croquet balls. If you don't have different colored balls, key them with markers. The object of the game is to hit the balls through all of the wickets in a set order. When a player's ball strikes another ball, he or she can knock the opponent's ball away and go again.

For an added challenge, lay the course out from room to room and under furniture. Now that's a sticky wicket!

Indoor Sports

Sound Off in Print

Does your child have something important on his or her mind? Then why not have him or her write a letter to the "editor" (you) about it?

Required:
Writing supplies

Have your child choose a subject that he or she feels strongly about and offer in writing his or her position about an issue or a solution to a problem.

Once you've read your child's letter, write an "editor's note." You can express your agreement or disagreement with your child's point of view and add your thoughts on the matter. Give your child a chance to rebut (in print, of course). Then have your child take over as editor and write your own letter to him or her.

Don't be afraid to cover offbeat matters as well as the serious, like how to get the elephants in the zoo to eat their peanuts more quietly.

Great
Correspondence

Step Toss

Required:

Writing supplies, tape, rubber ball

This simple ball-toss activity will have your children doing some quick arithmetic while having quick fun on a cabin-bound day.

The object of the game is to toss a rubber ball up a flight of stairs so it bounces back, hitting as many steps as possible on the way down. Before the game, the players print numbers on sheets of paper and tape them to the front of each step to indicate the point value.

Each player stands at the bottom of the stairs and tosses the ball up. As the ball comes back down, the player adds up the numbers assigned to the steps it bounces on; the more bounces the higher the score.

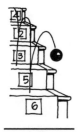

For a more challenging game, alternate between two different colors of paper on the steps, designating one as "add points" and the other as "subtract points." Younger children can enjoy the game as well by simply counting the number of bounces.

OK, get set to watch the bouncing ball. . . .

Indoor Sports

Storybook Bingo

Here's a version of bingo sure to inspire a beginning reader or group of players while generating a few belly laughs.

Make bingo cards by drawing a four-by-four-square grid (for a total of sixteen squares) on a piece of blank paper or thin cardboard. Ask the players to list common words that you or they can write in the squares. Stick with words that appear frequently in children's storybooks, such as "for," "yes," "I," "go," "boy," and "girl." Be sure that the children place the words randomly so that every card is different.

Have the players cut bingo markers out of colored paper with safety scissors, then begin reading a selected story. The children then listen for the words on their cards and place a marker on each word that they hear. The first one who places four markers on his or her card in a straight line in any direction shouts *bingo!* When that happens, remove the markers, swap cards, and get back to the story.

Required:

Writing supplies, white paper or thin cardboard, colored paper, safety scissors, favorite books

Fun and Games

Storybook Treasure Hunt

Required:

Books, writing supplies, prize or treat

Optional:

Magazines and newspapers

Here's a new twist on a scavenger hunt that young readers will have fun with as they follow clues from their favorite books. Lead your children to a hidden prize by giving them written clues that rely on books with which they're familiar and you have in your home. Each clue should relate to something from one of the familiar books to lead your child to an object in your home. For example:

Goldilocks sat on one on page 10 could be a hint to look on the rocking chair for the next clue.

Madeline was in one on page 23 might lead your kids to a bed.

Look for something the color of Max's boat could direct them to a red piece of paper after they check in Sendak's classic *Where the Wild Things Are*.

Older children can use magazines and newspapers. For younger kids, simply give them the clues, directing them to picture books that they know very well.

Any ideas for a clue from *Harold and the Purple Crayon*? That should lead to some interesting places. . . .

Fun and Games

Stuffed-Animal Show

Silly stuffed-animal tricks? You bet, and they're all on tape in your video camera.

Have your child gather several of his or her stuffed animals (if possible, choosing the most talented of the lot). Then give your child a chance to rehearse various acts with the creatures. Perhaps Teddy can walk on a rolling ball and Babar the elephant can do somersaults, back flips, handstands, and other gymnastic exercises, despite his size.

Get the camera ready, cue your child, then let the tape roll while the "performers" go through their paces. Your child can also explain to the video audience how he or she trained the animals, and give the creatures' names and backgrounds.

And don't worry if the "talent" makes a mistake or two on the air; that's to be expected in a live production.

Required:
Video camera, stuffed animals

Lights, Camera, Action!

Subminiature Golf

Required:

Marbles,
Popsicle sticks,
corrugated
cardboard,
boxes

Optional:

Hard foam
sheets, double-
stick tape or
nontoxic glue,
cardboard
tubes, small
toys, paint,
blocks

Here's a plan for big fun with a small version of an old family favorite. It's miniature golf with marbles and Popsicle sticks instead of golf balls and putters.

Your children can use the Popsicle sticks as is for putters, or they can glue on a shorter piece of stick or a rectangle of hard foam for the putter head. Use a large piece of corrugated cardboard for the golf course (two or more pieces can be taped together to get the desired size) and place it on several uniformly tall boxes to elevate it off the floor. Then cut holes in it slightly larger than the diameter of the marbles (remember, marbles may not be suitable for younger children).

Have your children add decorations (perhaps paint the areas around the holes green) and obstacles to the course. Obstacles can include cardboard tubes to putt through, blocks for bumpers, and, of course, plastic animals, figurines, and plastic dinos or space people to create the feel of a true miniature golf course.

Indoor Sports

Superior Supermarket

You and your child can enjoy doing the food shopping together, especially when the supermarket is in your own home.

Have your child create a grocery store, complete with various departments: fruits and vegetables, the freezer section, the deli counter, and so on. Your child can draw food items or cut pictures from magazines and supermarket circulars for the grocery stock. Empty cardboard boxes can represent "packaged" goods (pasta, cereals, etc.). Be sure to make play currency too.

Once your child has stocked the supermarket with his or her favorite foods, you can select some products by putting them into a basket, bag, or box. And, while you're shopping, your child can conduct taste tests, sell you on a new food, or demonstrate a new recipe.

Finally, head over to the cash register and let your child ring up your order. Then, you can have your child switch roles with you and take a whirl at shopping—provided you've left any food on the shelves, that is!

Required:

Food products (or their empty containers), magazines and supermarket circulars, scissors, basket, bag or box

Optional:

Play currency, cooking and serving supplies

Main Street

Sweepstakes Surprises

Required:

Art and writing supplies, envelopes

I s your family on a lucky streak? Then have your child enter each family member in a homespun lottery.

Your child can make a variety of prizes such as drawings, modeling-clay sculptures, greeting cards, and poems. (Make sure he or she makes enough items so that everybody gets one.) Then have your child write the prize names on slips of paper (one prize per page) and put each in a separate envelope. Mix up the envelopes and place one under each family member's dinner plate.

Instead of homemade prizes, older children might substitute "service coupons" (slips of paper that entitle the bearer to such gifts as "breakfast in bed," "reading a story," and "closet cleaning"). The recipient gets to decide on a time to redeem the prize.

Fun and Games

After dinner (or at another appropriate time when the rest of the family is at home), have participants take turns opening the envelopes and reading their prizes aloud. Your child can present the homemade gifts and elaborate on the service prizes. Isn't it great when everyone is a winner?

Tetherball Bowling

This activity adds a new swing to bowling. Instead of rolling a ball to try to knock over the pins, your child swings a wiffle or foam ball suspended from a string.

To start, you need to prepare a ball for hanging in a doorway from a long piece of string, if you're using a foam ball, push a needle and thread through the surface and tie it in a loop to connect the string (your job). Attach the string to the top of the door frame with packaging tape or a thumbtack so that the ball hangs about two inches above the floor.

When the ball setup is complete, have your child place one or more toilet paper tubes on the floor and try to knock them over by gently swinging the ball at them.

For variety, suggest the following: arranging the targets in different patterns, stacking them in pyramids, or even lining them up close to each other and trying to knock over just one tube at a time.

One thing is certain: Once your child gets in the swing of this game, he or she will truly have a ball.

Required:

String, wiffle or foam ball (foam ball requires needle and thread), thumbtack or tape, toilet paper tubes

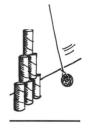

Indoor Sports

Time Capsule

Required:

Cardboard box or oatmeal container, toilet paper tubes, tape, string, pipe cleaners, recycled materials, art supplies

Congratulations! You and your child have just discovered a most unusual time capsule right in your living room.

Fill a "time capsule" (a cardboard box or oatmeal container) with unusual items, such as a toilet paper tube festooned with several pipe cleaners and rubber bands, a chopstick with a string taped to the end, or two bottle caps taped together and wrapped in recycled aluminum foil. Your anthropologist/child can then sift through the contents, assign names to each item, explain what the various artifacts were used for, and speculate about the civilization that created them.

When your child has offered hypotheses about all the gizmos, let him or her create the contents for another capsule. Provide plenty of supplies (cardboard tubes, containers, etc.) so that he or she can try to stump you when it's your turn to identify the goodies.

All right, the idea behind the hydrogen-fusion can opener is clear. But we still aren't sure about what appear to be solar-powered ear lamps. . . .

Imagine This

Toys Galore

There's always room for a new toy store in the neighborhood. In fact, you and your child can open one anytime in your own home.

Have your child assemble some of his or her favorite toys and games in the "showroom." To add to the inventory, your child might want to make some toys (such as plastic-spoon puppets, paper-bag masks, cardboard-box building blocks, Lego creations, etc.). Suggest that the toy-store proprietor group his or her wares according to type. For instance, board games can go in one "aisle," dolls in a second, building blocks and Legos in another, etc.

When the store is ready to open for business, you can be the proud first customer, and your child can guide you around, demonstrating how the toys work, giving sales pitches, answering technical and pricing questions, and ringing up purchases.

Of course, you might want to switch roles after a while to give your child a chance to shop. What child doesn't enjoy visiting a toy store?

Required:
Toys

Optional:
Recycled materials

Main Street

Trailblazers

Required:

Socks, writing supplies

Optional:

Prize or treat

Kids get a kick out of following trail markers through the woods. This plan for an indoor hike gives your child a chance to follow the trail and to make new paths of his or her own. Best of all, he or she can be back in the kitchen for lunch or dinner.

You can mark the first trail for your hiker to follow by strategically placing socks as you weave along through rooms and hallways. Each sock should always be within sight of the previous one. Work with your child to create some simple rules, like having the toe of each sock always point to the next marker.

You can also add variety by turning the hike into a treasure hunt. Simply write clues on pieces of paper to put inside the socks that will direct your child to hidden treasures along the way: For example, "Proceed three more markers and find a large square object four paces from the trail."

After your explorer successfully follows your trail through the house, have him or her mark a route for you to follow. Now hit the trail, there's adventure ahead. . . .

Fun and Games

Tube Heads

This activity, which allows your child to produce and talk back to TV shows, might be the only type of "interactive television" we'll ever endorse and enjoy.

Required:

Large cardboard box, art supplies, yogurt container lids, glue or tape, straws

To make some "tube head" gear, take a box at least 12 by 12 by 18 inches, and cut out a "screen" in front, as well as a hole in the bottom large enough for a person's head to comfortably fit through. Have your child draw a dial or two under the screen, or affix yogurt container lids; these are the "controls." In back of the "set," tape two drinking straws at a 45-degree angle to each other (the antennae).

Next, have your child make a TV listing, including the program titles and types (documentaries, cartoons, news, etc.) and segment descriptions. "Audience" members then take turns choosing the shows for your tube head child to "broadcast" (act out). For added fun, groups of kids can wear their own tube head gear and become part of the show.

This is one—and perhaps the only—time when you're sure to find "talking heads" great television!

Fun and Games

Tube Sculpture

Required:

Used containers, packing and other nonrecyclable materials, art supplies, nontoxic glue and tape

Optional:

Marbles

Artists sometimes use castoff objects, old car parts, and an assortment of things otherwise destined for the junkyard to create their sculptures. Check out your recycling bin the next time your child is in the mood for a sculpting project.

Gather up cardboard tubes, chunks of foam, nonrecyclable containers, and paper, as well as glue and tape. For a simple and stable sculpture, a younger child can use a cardboard box as a base, then attach other objects to it with the glue and tape.

For additional fun, suggest that your child incorporate a marble chute into whatever sculpture piece he or she is creating (keep a close watch on younger siblings). Perhaps you'll be in the vanguard of a new art form: Art de Chute.

Whatever kinds of sculpture pieces your child makes, line them up in the playroom so everyone can enjoy a good old homemade sculpture garden.

Arts & Crafts

Tunnel Vision

Here's a simple "find-the-object" game that will tantalize cabin-bound kids of all ages.

Required:
Paper towel tube, magazines and other photo sources

All you need to play is a paper towel tube. Clip a large photograph from a magazine or newspaper or draw one yourself, then have your children scan it with the tube in search of a specific item that you call out (say, a green square on a drawing you made or a flower in a photograph).

You can boost the challenge for older kids by selecting more complex photographs and more subtle items or by reducing the opening at the far end of the tube with tape. Even more difficult is using the tube to view a picture that they haven't seen before, then trying to imagine and describe the picture in its entirety.

Yet another variation involves scanning the room for certain items. For instance, "look for a plus sign (+)" might mean the spot on the couch where the cushions all come together or a pattern on the floor tiles. Again, you can easily vary the difficulty to match the activity to a particular child's age and abilities.

Maybe your kids *will* spot the proverbial light at the end of the tunnel. . . .

Fun and Games

Two-Bit Tiddlywinks

Required:

Coins, spoons, cup or bowl

Tiddlywinks is an old favorite that involves snapping plastic disks into a target cup. Here's a do-it-yourself version that takes just small change to put together.

The idea of the game is to use a spoon to flip coins into a cup or bowl placed in the center of the table. Place the coins on the handle of a spoon, with the handle pointing away from the target. Gently tap the spoon so that the coin is launched into the air toward the target. After demonstrating how the launcher works, have the players experiment with different coins and different spoons to find the best combination.

For variety, add smaller and larger targets and assign a point value to each, the smaller the target the higher the points.

One thing you can be sure of: Your children will flip when they get their two cents in!

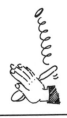

Fun and Games

Two-Dimensional Dollhouse

Are your kids ready for a home of their own? Maybe not, but this simple on-the-wall dollhouse can make for some off-the-wall fun.

Required:

Large sheet of paper, art supplies, nontoxic glue, tape

Begin by helping your children draw a cutaway view of a house on a large piece of paper. You can also have them draw outside scenery as viewed through the windows. When the house is ready, tape it to a wall and your junior interior decorators can get to work.

Have your children draw and color furniture, knickknacks, pets, and people to put in the house. They can try to make rooms that match their own homes or create the bedroom of their dreams. Encourage them to include small details to make their house look more like a home: dishes on the table, or a stack of magazines scattered on the coffee table, and so on.

How about that! Your kids not only made their bed, they made their whole house!

Arts & Crafts

Video Biography

Required:
Video camera

Isn't it nice to hear life stories of family members in their own words? Why not have your child conduct a biographical interview with siblings or friends? Here are some sample questions to begin with for younger and older subjects:

For Younger Subjects

Who's in your family? Who are your friends? What's your favorite playtime activity? Which books and songs do you like best? What is your favorite thing at school? Which color do you like the most?

For Older Subjects

Were you named for anyone? Where did you grow up? What were your favorite things to do as a child? How have things changed since you were a child? What is the funniest thing that's ever happened to you? What advice can you give to others?

Encourage your child to think of more questions to ask, including follow-up questions during the interview. He or she can also create an autobiographical tape by answering the same interview questions on camera.

Take one!

Lights, Camera, Action!

Wacky Warm-Ups

Before your young athletes start any of their indoor sports events, get them properly warmed up with these silly stretches and crazy calisthenics. Remember, though, the main idea here is to stretch your kids' enjoyment!

To begin, pick someone to be the exercise leader (be sure to have the children change places often). It's the leader's task to come up with the stretches. Here are some starter ideas:

Finger flexes. "Fingers of both hands together; push and up and down. Again!"

Elbow flaps. "Strut like a chicken!"

Tongue stretches. "Stick out those tongues! You can do it; touch your nose!"

Eyebrow lifts. "Everyone together now; open your eyes WIDE and lift those lazy eyebrows!"

Toe wiggles. "Get those toes moving! Wiggle and waggle and spread and scrunch!"

Nostril flares. "Open and shut and open and shut!"

Moms and Dads, time to join the kids and S-T-R-E-T-C-H your fun too!

Indoor Sports

Wall Mural

Required:

Large sheets of paper, masking tape, art supplies

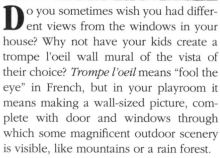

Do you sometimes wish you had different views from the windows in your house? Why not have your kids create a trompe l'oeil wall mural of the vista of their choice? *Trompe l'oeil* means "fool the eye" in French, but in your playroom it means making a wall-sized picture, complete with door and windows through which some magnificent outdoor scenery is visible, like mountains or a rain forest.

Begin by taping pieces of paper together to form a larger sheet to tape to the wall. Have your kids decide what they want to draw, then perhaps start with a light pencil sketch of their idea before adding color. In addition to including a window or door on their mural, your children might add other details to make it look like part of the room.

For instance, they can draw a picture on the picture, complete with a frame. They can also add touches like a crack in the wall, a light switch, or "paintings of paintings" and other artwork.

Or suggest this one: a magic button that, when pressed, will instantly clean up a playroom and make the sun come out!

Arts & Crafts

Welcoming Committee

All family members like a hearty welcome home, even if they've only been away for the school or work day, a half-hour errand, or a ten-minute excursion to shovel the walk.

Required:

Poster board or a roll of paper (or paper bags), art supplies

Supply your child with large sheets of paper or poster board and art supplies to make welcome-home signs that can be placed near the door. For banners, provide a role of wide paper or have your child tape together sheets of paper or flat sections of paper bags.

Young children can draw pictures for the person who's been "away," while older kids can write greetings such as: "Hope you caught some rays while you were gone today." "We missed you so much while you went to the store!" "Hope you had fun during gym today."

In any case, encourage silliness! The shorter the amount of time a particular person was away from the house, the more earnest should be the welcome message and greeting ritual. Speaking of which, welcome back from your walk around the block with the dog; everyone missed you a lot!

Arts & Crafts

What a Character!

Required:

Costumes, props, accessories

Here's a proven cabin-fever buster designed for a child who enjoys dress-up games.

Gather some accessories (hats, gloves, jewelry, scarves, etc.), clothing (oversized shirts, socks, shoes, and the like), and a variety of props (a briefcase, a newspaper, sports equipment, and so on). Then have your child hop "onstage" (a space you designate for the performance). Now give your child an item or two. He or she can put on the "costume" (or hold it, if appropriate) and undergo a theatrical transformation.

Have your child introduce him- or herself, give basic facts (name, age, place of residence), and elaborate on his or her background. (Your child might also sing a song or tell a story in character.)

You can ask the character questions to reveal additional information. And be sure to find out why he or she is wearing your child's favorite sweatshirt. . . .

Performances

What's Your Opinion?

Although you and your child may not see eye to eye on every issue, you can still listen to each other's point of view. Choose a lighthearted "controversy," such as which pizza topping is best.

Have your child state and then back up his or her position (for example, perhaps your child favors pepperoni for its nice smooth edges). Counter his or her opinion with your own (you might tout the virtues of double-cheese: its calcium content, mellow flavor, and stringiness).

Give your child a chance to respond, then offer him or her a counterpoint, and so on. Are you ready to give the activity a twist? Switch positions with your child and begin again. See how well each of you can back up the "opposing" point of view (using original arguments or elaborating on each other's ideas).

Have either of you been swayed to the other camp's position on pizza toppings? Well, it *is* a child's (or is that "parent's"?) prerogative to change his or her mind.

Fun and Games

White House Improv

Required:

Desk and chair

Optional:

Writing supplies

What's it like to be in both the limelight and the hot seat? Just ask the president!

Design an Oval Office at your home (with a real or make-believe desk and chair, as well as a designated place for reporters). Then have your child role-play the president and field questions from the press (play-acted by you and any other participants). You can make a list of questions in advance with your child's help, including a range of topics from education to health care. For variation, you can also pose questions involving your neighborhood (such as how you might get your neighborhood to recycle cardboard and more plastics) that normally don't fall under the president's jurisdiction.

Fire the questions at the "prez" one at a time and see what kind of thoughtful answers or bluff he or she provides. Then switch places with your child: You be the president and take on the media. Have your child jot down notes about your responses; perhaps he or she can use them to write tomorrow's front-page news story about the press conference.

Performances

Witches' Brew

▶Adult Supervision

Required:
Common cooking ingredients, bowls, spoons, measuring cups, and other utensils

Eye of newt, tongue of frog, turtle's breath, and moss from log. How come *imaginary* witches and magicians have all the fun? Your kids can concoct their own magic potions right in the kitchen.

Provide your kids with a variety of ingredients: spices, flour, cornstarch, pasta, ketchup, mustard, oil, cracker crumbs, stale bread, food coloring, vinegar and baking soda (to add "fizz"). Also needed are bowls, spoons, a whisk, and measuring cups. Now turn them loose, and remember, the more disgusting their concoction the better!

Encourage your children to be "scientific" about their magic by measuring carefully and adding the ingredients at just the "right" time. To get in the true witches' brew spirit, ask them to describe their ingredients (mustard might be extract of bird feather) and the kind of magic the potion will make. Will it turn the cat into a dinosaur, make someone invisible, or melt a hole in the ground for a swimming pool?

Stir a bowl of gruesome mix, this witches' brew will work some tricks. . . .

Fun and Games

Word Gymnasts

Required:

Thesaurus or synonym dictionary, writing supplies

Would you believe that the sentence "The dog dug up his old bone from the yard, then brought it into the house for everyone to see" can be the source of great entertainment? All you need is a thesaurus or book of synonyms.

First, your child will need a list of sentences; make them up or cull them from magazines or books. Then provide the thesaurus and have your child try to find as many lofty-sounding replacements for the words in the sentence as possible. Take turns reading the sentences aloud and perhaps write the most intriguing on a large sheet of poster board or paper so other family members can enjoy them.

As a variation, have your child try to substitute haughty terms for the words in the first paragraph or two of a newspaper article, magazine story, or book. Either way, have your child read his or her versions aloud to you.

As for the sentence about Rover in the first paragraph above, try this: "The canine excavated his superannuated skeletal structure from the cloister garth, then transported it into the domicile for one and all to behold."

Fun and Games

Word Swap

Here's a game that can add a little silliness to a favorite book and entertain your cabin-bound child at the same time.

Required:

Writing supplies, favorite books

To prepare, help your child come up with twenty or so common nouns and write them on slips of paper. Names of familiar objects work best, so your slips might include "dog," "cat," "banana," "car," "sink," and other similar words. Fold the slips of paper and put them in a bowl, pick a favorite book, and let the fun begin.

As you're reading, have your child pull paper slips from the bowl for use as substitutes to nouns in the story. You can try a substitution for every common noun in the story or simply substitute the words as the mood strikes you. Once a substitution is made, use the new word each time the original word comes up in the story. The challenge will be to keep reading through the giggles.

Jack's mother was furious. "I told you to sell our **pajamas** so we could get **frogs** to eat! Instead, you bring home a sack of magic **boots**!" She threw the **boots** out the window and sent Jack to his room. The next morning, he awoke to find that the **boots** had grown into giant **bananas**!

Fun and Games

World Atlas

Required:

Art and writing supplies, stapler, binder or report cover

Optional:

Encyclopedias, globes, computer programs and other reference sources,

A completely new and revised atlas is about to hit the bookshelves, and the author is your child.

If your child is a geography buff, organizing all he or she knows about states, countries, continents, oceans, rivers, mountains, and so on into book form should be a pleasant cabin-fever buster. Your child can check reference materials (encyclopedias, globes, computer programs, textbooks, etc.) that you have in your home to supplement his or her (and your) knowledge to create maps of the world.

Or your child can "wing it," creating drawings that approximate the real things (you and your child can always revise the maps later after a visit to the public library). And if your child is also an astronomy aficionado, he or she can include star maps showing the relationship of the earth to other planets in the solar system.

Finally, encourage your junior cartographer to add some descriptive text about the features of the world; you'll have to read it to believe it!

Create-a-Book

Your John Hancock

If you and your child weren't asked to sign the Declaration of Independence, cheer up; you can scrawl your names in endless ways on an infinite variety of documents anytime the mood strikes you.

Required:
Writing supplies

Have your child write his or her name in such a way that the signature reflects various moods (excited, scared, joyous, etc.), a season, or a special activity (running, jumping, and so on). You can specify what the signature is supposed to reflect, or you can try to guess which feeling, place, or thing your child had in mind when he or she was signing on the bottom line. You might also have your child create signatures for various storybook characters.

For example, perhaps David Copperfield writes his name in small, neat letters while Mr. Micawber's signature takes up three-quarters of a page. If you have a handwriting sleuth at home, you can have him or her identify the signatures of several name-signers. Naturally, the writers will have to disguise their real signatures to fool your resident expert.

Fun and Games

Required:

Large box (or old sheet and chairs), scissors

Some people think that commercial television is pretty zany as it is, with inane plots that appear to be written by a visitor from another planet and commercials designed to transform our children into toy and junk-food addicts.

But there's hope if you produce your own "Cabin-Fever Television Special." Cut out a square from a large box (an appliance box works well, or set up four chairs in a square, drape an expendable sheet over them, and cut out the picture "screen").

Now have your child climb in and describe for you and other cabin-bound children the best way to spend time during wintry or rainy days or days when you're not feeling so good. Perhaps he or she can put on a commercial demonstrating the best rainy-day toys to play with.

Take note: You'll probably gain some great insights into what your kids want to do when they're cabin-bound or sick. And there's another benefit, too: When your kids are *inside* the tube, you don't have to worry about them passing their time *in front of* the real one-eyed monster.

Performances

Index

Activities Suited to Younger Kids

Great Correspondence

207

Sound Works